T0283296

What Iranians Want

ARASH AZIZI

WHAT IRANIANS WANT

WOMEN, LIFE, FREEDOM

ONEWORLD

A Oneworld Book

First published by Oneworld Publications in 2024

ISBN 978-0-86154-711-1
eISBN 978-0-86154-712-8

Typeset by Geethik Technologies
Printed and bound in Great Britain by Clays Ltd, Elcograf S.p.A.

Oneworld Publications
10 Bloomsbury Street
London WC1B 3SR
England

Stay up to date with the latest books,
special offers, and exclusive content from
Oneworld with our newsletter

Sign up on our website
oneworld-publications.com

For my fellow Iranians

'Oh, of who do I speak?

We live without reason,

They are conscious of the reason for their death.'

— Ahmad Shamlu

'And yet, the country of my childhood lives within me with a primacy that is a form of love.'

— Eva Hoffman

Table of Contents

Foreword

In autumn 2022, thousands of protesters chanted on the streets of Iran 'Don't call this a protest. This is a revolution.' It had started as a protest against the brutal killing of one young woman at the hands of the police. Over 2022 and 2023, it morphed into an all-out cry for change – a challenge the regime still can't fully contain. After decades of despotism, Iranians have still not stopped fighting for themselves, their nation, their future.

They have not given up, despite odds so bad no gambler would bet on them. Before September 2022 it seemed Iran was an exhausted country. The economic outlook was bleak: for four years running it boasted inflation higher than 30%. Young people struggled to find jobs in the fields for which they were qualified. Compulsory Hijab had been in place for over forty years. The last significant wave of protests, at the tail-end of 2019, became notorious as 'Bloody November' – a title earned in the deaths of over a thousand protesters.

And yet, after the death of Mahsa Amini, Iranians rose up, undaunted by the disappointments and defeats of previous years. Their courage came from thousands of small acts of resistance – the female singer in Tabriz performing regardless of an official ban, the activists who continue to speak out from prison cells, the filmmakers defying the censors and distributing their films underground. And, moreover, young women, some even teenagers, joined the streets en masse.

Who were these women awing the world with their courage, publicly burning their headscarves? The Iranian security forces were not a force to be taken lightly, hardened by their deployments in the civil wars in Iraq and Syria. Who were the ordinary Iranians daring to stand up to them, flipping the bird at pictures of their leader, Khamenei? Where had they come from?

Iran often makes the global headlines, but you can't find the answers to these questions there. Western commentators are more interested in its nuclear programme, involvement in proxy wars elsewhere in the region and its ballistic missile development. Where protests have been covered, journalists rarely probe beneath the surface of a battle between 'tradition' and 'modernity', a battle fought between hardline Islamists and Western liberals. These accounts may contain a grain of truth but they're not the full story. Iranians have bigger ambitions than that, and their struggles are richer and more diverse than the usual narratives tell us. So what do Iranians want?

This book is an attempt to answer this question. Born in 1988 in Tehran, I come from a generation of Iranians whose life has been defined by dashed hopes for reform and progress. One of my earliest political memories was the election of President Khatami in 1997 – a reformist candidate who swept to a landslide victory on the backs of young people and women, hopeful for his political programme. Khatami's failure proved to be one in a long line of defeats: the 2009 Green Movement against a stolen election; the nuclear deal of 2015 and forlorn hopes about the possibility of it opening Iran's doors to the world; the series of uprisings in 2017–18, 2019–2020 and ultimately 2022–2023. Every protest movement since has been crushed in blood. Having left Iran in 2008, I've witnessed much of this from afar. But I've never lost my solidarity with those resisting in my homeland.

This isn't a top-down political history, tracing the ebbs and flows of popular protest since the Islamic Republic was founded in 1979. Instead, this is a window into the aspirations of Iranians risking everything for change *now* – and the many decades that forged their will to act. I want to show you what Iranians want and *why* they are fighting for it. Each battle I focus on, from the fight against compulsory Hijab, to freedom of expression, to conservation of the Persian cheetah, has deep roots in modern Iranian history. The slogan 'Women, Life, Freedom' unifies all these issues – transforming demands into a programme. In painting a portrait of this movement, and paying tribute to its predecessors, I want to make the voices of Iranians heard loud and clear throughout a world that so often ignores them.

Since September 2022, I have followed the events of my homeland with hope and trepidation in equal measure. I don't know what the next chapter will hold, although I have tried to imagine what it could look like. The arc of history, sadly, doesn't always bend toward justice. The visionaries fighting for change today may not see that change in their lifetimes; there may be many more martyrs under the banner Women, Life, Freedom but few concrete victories. Hal Draper, an American revolutionary, once wrote 'Nothing can be guaranteed, of course, except the honour and dignity of fighting for a new and better world, rather than the vileness of adapting one's mind and heart to a vile one.' Through their actions, in September 2022 and in every protest before and after, Iranians have shown they want this honour and dignity. Even if the current movement falls, the torch will be passed on and the flame will not die. A better Iran remains the ultimate goal, for which every generation will fight.

One

Freedom is Global: The Fight Against Compulsory Hijab

One September afternoon in 2022, a young woman got off at a metro stop in Tehran. A week short of her twenty-second birth-day, Mahsa Amini was from a Kurdish family in the western Iranian town of Saqqez. She had come to the capital to shop and have fun, like so many young women do. As she came up the steps of Martyr Haqqani station, she could glimpse the verdant woods of Taleqani park, one of Tehran's most spectacular green spaces, studded with pine and mulberry trees. It was an oasis of calm for Mahsa, amid the city's chaos. Her brother, Kiarash, would later say: 'We are strangers to this city.'[1] It was hard to feel at ease in the swarming metropolis as an outsider.

Tuesday 13 September would be far from a calm day for Mahsa. Outside the station, she was spotted by the white-and-green vans of the Guidance Patrol, the dreaded wing of Iranian police's Moral Security Division, dispatched to detain women with 'bad or inadequate Hijab'. Her Hijab, apparently, didn't cut the mustard. They threw her into the van, along with other women who had failed to pass a wholly arbitrary appearance test. It would take them to a nearby detention centre on Vozara Street, where women arrested for 'bad Hijab' had to undergo re-education and sign a pledge to observe the 'Islamic' dress code. At the very least, this would ruin her trip, so she protested, alongside a few others. The Patrol didn't take kindly to her complaints, and brutally beat her during the ten-minute journey. Shortly after arriving at the centre, she fainted and was taken to the nearby Kasra Hospital. By 8:30 p.m. that night, she was declared brain-dead, even though her heart was still beating. By Friday, she was dead. She would never see her twenty-second birthday.

Mahsa had not come to Tehran to be a hero. She was not there to make history; she had no plans of making a stand like Rosa Parks. She was there to celebrate her birthday and to prepare for her enrolment at the University of Urumiyah in northwestern Iran, where she had been admitted recently.[2] She was simply a young woman who wanted to enjoy herself.

Mahsa, called Jina by her family, had no way of knowing that her funeral in Saqqez on Saturday would be attended by thousands, shouting 'Death to the dictator'. 'Your Name Will Become a Sign', the epitaph on her gravestone chosen by her mother, would inspire hundreds of thousands of Iranians who would launch a revolution in her honour. Her name would become the most tweeted hashtag in the history of the internet. Mahsa Amini would not have wanted any of this. Like George Floyd, she only wanted to live.

Her murder touched a nerve precisely because so many Iranian women knew it could have been them. By all accounts, she was hardly in violation of the Hijab rules. Pictures and videos that later circulated showed an ordinary Iranian woman. When outside, she wore long, loose, dark cloaks, with a bit of hair jutting out of the mandatory veil. Inside, she wore colourful, embroidered dresses, dancing to Kurdish music and Persian divas alike.

Yet she had been killed simply because she resisted the capricious rule of the thugs of the Islamic Republic, even if only for a few minutes. Iranians of all walks of life were outraged. Even those who chose to veil much more strictly knew that this could happen to a niece, cousin or sister who did not.

Iranians rose up in unprecedented numbers. Protests spread around every corner of the country. The Kurdish slogan 'Women, Life, Freedom', cried in chorus at the initial protests in Saqqez and other Kurdish cities, now echoed through every street in Iran. It encapsulated everything Iranians were fighting for.

Following an ancient Iranian tradition, women cut their hair to signal mourning. Many around the world imitated the gesture in solidarity. Not for the first or last time, young Iranian girls and women astounded the world by their display of courage. They burnt their mandatory headscarves as they danced on the streets and threw them onto bonfires. At school after school, they gave the middle finger to the omnipresent pictures of the Supreme Leader Ayatollah Khamenei and his predecessor Ayatollah Khomeini, whose museum-house in Khomein was also set on fire.[3] Protesters started chanting: 'Don't call this a revolt. This is a revolution.' The unthinkable was happening. And women were at the forefront.

It took the world by surprise. But it had been a long time in the making.

* * *

By the time of Mahsa's state murder, Iranian women had had to endure more than four decades of compulsory veiling. This policy, which forces women to cover all their body except for the face and the palm of their hands, doesn't have parallels anywhere in the world, Muslim or otherwise. Only the legally unrecognised Taliban regime enforces an equivalent rule. Even Saudi Arabia, known for the most drastic application of Islamic law, never actually enforced Hijab all over its territory. In 2019, the Saudi Arabian government announced the end of the mandatory Hijab, and you can now see unveiled women on streets and billboards in Riyadh and Jeddah. Iran stands out as a shocking outlier.

Standing out had always been the point. The men (and they were mostly men) who built the Islamic Republic after 1979 could genuinely boast of its uniqueness. In the midst of the Cold War, the new republic didn't mimic the capitalist West or the socialist East, nor did its path follow the experiences of postcolonial revolutionary states such as Algeria or Syria, or even other nominal 'Islamic Republics' in neighbouring Afghanistan or Pakistan. The new republic was led not by a typical politician, general or ex-guerilla but by an octogenarian, high-ranking cleric with strong mystical inclinations. Ayatollah Ruhollah Khomeini's blueprint for a new form of Islamist governance owed less to any real-life example than it did to Plato's Philosopher King. Only he called it the Guardian Jurist, better known in English as the Supreme Leader. From his perch as the first ever Guardian Jurist of Iran, the uncompromising Khomeini wanted to do something more than changing laws or governments. He wanted to fundamentally reshape life in Iran to conform to his idea of Islam. Muslim reformers had, for decades, attempted to reconcile their faith and its ideals with the necessities of their age. Khomeini would have none of that. His government was to be Islamic, as he understood it, 'not a word more, not a word less'.

Women in Iran of 1979 seemed to stand in the way of Khomeini's vision by their very existence. This even applied to devout Muslims. Like believers across the world, they interpreted and observed religious rules in myriad ways. Some wore the long, all-encompassing black chador, some didn't. Some wore more relaxed versions of Hijab like a little scarf (*roosari*) that covered some of their hair. Some only wore the Hijab when they visited religious shrines. Some only wore it during the holy month of Ramadan. Some only wore it when they prayed; which could be five times a day or once in a blue moon. Maryam, then a young woman in the city of Arak, remembers mail-ordering the latest fashionable miniskirts (or *minijupe*, as they were known by their French name) or cleavage-showing *décolleté* blouses; she wore those on outings, far from the prying eyes of her devout parents. But she also wore her chador when she occasionally prayed to ask God for something she desired, or on trips to Mashhad to visit the shrine of Reza, the only Shia Imam buried in Iran. Others showed similar flexibility.[4]

Whatever their religious preferences, the women of 1979 enjoyed the progressive changes brought about by the tireless work of Iranian feminists in the preceding decades. This included the Family Protection Act of 1975, which raised the minimum age for marriage and gave women an equal right to divorce, making Iran's laws among the most progressive in the Global South.[5] Iranian women now served as judges, members of parliament, cabinet ministers, diplomats, university professors, doctors and engineers. Overcoming the gender segregation that was previously the norm in many spheres, Iranian women shared workspaces, university classes, cinemas, beaches and dance clubs with men. Women were active citizens, and many of them joined the protests against the Shah that culminated in the 1979 revolution.

Khomeini's vision left no room for Iranian women as they actually lived their lives. This wasn't a surprise to anybody who had followed his career. In 1963 he had opposed female suffrage and called on people to 'express your disgust at equality of rights, of women's participation in society which will come with endless corruption'.[6] A year later, he had protested the hiring of female teachers for male high schools and added that 'insisting on women joining the government institutions is corrupt and pointless'.[7]

To build his ideal society, Khomeini needed to deal with the women.

* * *

On 23 January 1979, as the Grand Ayatollah whiled away the last days of his Parisian exile, he did something he had never done before: he gave an interview to a female reporter.[8] The twenty-six-year-old Nooshabeh Amiri was a walking embodiment of the advances made by the Iranian women in the preceding decades. She held a BA in journalism and an MA in psychology and had been a professional reporter from the age of nineteen. In an environment where even progressive male intellectuals often expressed heavily sexist opinions, her presence as a top political journalist for Tehran's most popular daily, *Kayhan*, was telling. She often accompanied prime ministers on trips all over the country. Now, *Kayhan*'s editor, Rahman Hatefi, secretly a member of the communist Tudeh Party, had dispatched Nooshabeh to Paris for a historic task: interviewing Khomeini.

Khomeini had already spoken to dozens of journalists from around the world but his words were usually carefully translated by his advisors, schooled in the West, and watered down before they reached a wider audience. Now, for the first time, he spoke to the Tehran press, newly free to report on the revolution underway.

Nooshabeh wanted to sound conciliatory to a man clearly considered as a leader by millions while also articulating her concerns. She recalls feeling somewhat terrified in a room filled with men who were sitting on the ground, as was the tradition in Shia seminaries. With her long black hair and professional attire, Nooshabeh seemed out of place.

'You have accepted my presence as a woman,' she told Khomeini, 'and this shows this to be a progressive movement… Do you believe our women have to have the Hijab? Should they cover their hair?'

Khomeini smirked at the question and retorted: 'Who said I accepted your presence? I didn't. You came here yourself and I had no idea you were coming. This doesn't show that Islam is progressive. Yes, Islam is progressive but not as dreamed by some women. Progress has to do with human self-perfection, not going to the movies and dance clubs. This is the progress they made for you. They made you regress. We will have to undo this.'

Unperturbed, Nooshabeh pressed on. She asked what he thought about the fears that Iran was replacing the 'tyranny of jackboots' with 'tyranny of the clerics'. She could hear the men around her grow uncomfortable. How dare a young woman question the Grand Ayatollah himself? As the interview was cut short, they threatened her and told her to be careful with what she publishes.

Days before Khomeini's return to Tehran, months before the Islamic Republic's establishment, Nooshabeh knew that this man was up to no good. His mocking smirk gave the game away; the dismissive response only added insult to injury. Years later, she'd call it 'a poisonous smirk'. That night, as she read out the interview on the phone to her editor, Hatefi, she cried. 'A man full of spite and hate is coming to rule over us,' she said.

But her warnings fell on deaf ears. There was just no end to the wild clamouring for Khomeini. Some even claimed that his picture had appeared in the moon. Speaking on 29 January, Simin Daneshvar, one of Iran's top novelists, spoke of her support for Khomeini and said: 'I have read most of his statements and interviews and listened to most of his tapes. He has always said he will respect individual, social and political freedoms… I am optimistic.'

On 1 February, Khomeini came back to Iran, welcomed by millions who greeted him at the airport and listened to his landmark speech in Tehran's main cemetery. In less than two weeks, the Shah's last prime minister, the social democratic Shapour Bakhtiar, fled. Now the path was clear for Khomeini's Revolutionary Council to construct a new regime.

They wasted no time. Former government officials, including Farrokhroo Parsa, the first woman to serve in the cabinet, were put on trial, each lasting a handful of minutes. Then they were executed. A few brave women sounded the alarms. Nooshabeh was just one of them. But their efforts, even before Bakhtiar left the country, were to no avail.

While Bakhtiar still sat in the prime minister's office, Mahshid Amirshahi, a notable novelist, spoke of her astonishment at the readiness to sideline him. Bakhtiar's party, the left-leaning National Front, had kicked him out. The intellectual class, enamoured with Khomeini, had no time for Bakhtiar. On 6 February, writing for the liberal daily *Ayandegan*, Amirhshahi asked: 'Is there no one to support Bakhtiar?'[9] She warned that the intervention of clerics in politics would have disastrous consequences.

When Michel Foucault, the celebrated French philosopher, wrote about his admiration for Khomeini and the movement in Iran, an Iranian woman named Atoussa H. called him out in a public letter. 'Everywhere outside Iran, Islam serves as a cover for feudal or pseudo-revolutionary oppression,' she wrote. Foucault suggested she failed to approach Islam with even 'a minimum of intelligence'. Meanwhile his 'intelligence' extended to arguing that by 'Islamic government' no one possibly meant 'a political regime in which the clerics would have a role of supervision or control'.[10]

One of the first measures of the new order was the annulment of the Family Protection Act of 1975, which Khomeini regarded with special contempt. Women loudly protested this, but again they were mostly ignored. On 4 March, Soraya Sadr Danesh, Nooshabeh's colleague at *Kayhan*, published an editorial with a telling headline: 'Let's not forget the women.'[11]

'Out of all the incorrect and unjust laws, why go for annulling the Family Act?' she asked.

But Khomeini was just getting started, and already had a new target. He now announced a battle against what he saw as the pinnacle of 'corruption and prostitution': women without Hijab.

* * *

In the months leading to his triumphant return to Iran, Khomeini had cynically adopted the language of human rights and freedom to win over clueless Western observers. Even then, his real ideas were obvious if anyone cared to investigate, as Nooshabeh did.

Now ensconced in power, he launched his agenda for turning Iran into the Islamist land he had dreamed of. Even before the Islamic Republic had been established; even before Iranians could get a new constitution, Khomeini went on the offensive against women.

From his pulpit in the holy city of Qom, Khomeini criticised the fact that women were not donning the Hijab. On 1 March, he said: 'Islamic ministries shouldn't be a site of sin. In Islamic ministries, women shouldn't come out naked. Women can work but only if they wear the Hijab, Hijab, according to the Sharia.'[12]

On 6 March, he railed on: 'Islamic women are not dolls. They should come out with the Hijab. They shouldn't wear make-up. Women in government offices are still working in their previous attire. Women should change... They have reported to me that women still come out to work naked. This is against the Sharia. Women can participate in social affairs. But only with Islamic Hijab.'

As Iranian feminists prepared to hold a mass rally on International Women's Day, Sadegh Qotbzadeh, a confidante of Khomeini from his Parisian days and now head of the state broadcaster, denounced the occasion as 'Western' and promised that Iran would soon announce a new 'Islamic Women's Day'.[13]

Maryam Riazi, a well-known presenter from the pre-revolutionary days, appeared on TV to denounce the celebration of 8 March as a 'colonial and Western occasion'.[14] To the shock of her audience, she was, for the first time, veiled. The regime leaders had given her a simple choice: either cover up or you'll never be on TV again. Announcing the formation of the 'Women's Society of the Islamic Revolution', Riazi said the newly founded body 'declared that women who take part in such an event in the university or anywhere else are non-Muslims'.

The attacks on women didn't remain limited to speeches and TV announcements. Pro-Khomeini mobs, now self-styled as *Hezbollahis*, or Partisans of God, had already grown accustomed to attacking rallies of their opponents. At the sight of unveiled women at university campuses, Hezbollahis now used a new slogan: '*Ya Roosari, Ya* Toosari' (Cover your hair or be smacked on the head).

But nothing could cow the Iranian feminists who were intent on organising events for 8 March. They had even invited well-known feminists such as Kate Millett from the US to join in.[15] From France, Simone de Beauvoir sent her message of solidarity while a group of French feminists joined their Iranian sisters on the ground.

Alarmed by the new assault on their most basic rights, tens of thousands of women joined the feminist call for 8 March demonstrations. At the University of Tehran, 15,000 women listened to speeches before deciding to march. On a cold winter day, the streets of northern and central quarters of Tehran were flooded with thousands of women coalescing into a single march heading to the judiciary and the prime minister's office.

The demonstrators were not only students and political activists but women who never considered themselves radical until Khomeini's regime got going. They included female employees long used to the right to work and civic participation, which was now under threat. Among the marchers one could find employees of Iran Air and the Telecommunication Company, two of the best-known state corporations that were symbols of the modern Iran; there were nurses and doctors, teachers and school pupils. There was even a group of female employees of the Ministry of Foreign Affairs, diplomat feminists marching for the progress they had only recently won.

Although they were excoriated as counter-revolutionaries, many of these women had been at the forefront of the revolution against the Shah. Their slogans made this clear. 'We didn't make a revolution to go back in time,' they said. 'We will fight for freedom,' they said.

'Won't cover my hair, won't be smacked on the head.'
'We are opposed to tyranny.'
'We don't want the forced chador.'

But their most historic chant was a repurposing of a popular revolutionary slogan that had promised the new revolution would be 'neither Western, nor Eastern.' In response, women now shouted: 'Freedom is global – it's neither Western, nor Eastern.' Iranian women simultaneously affirmed their global sisterhood and highlighted the universal and transnational nature of their struggle. The revolution had promised to be a non-aligned Global South alternative to both capitalism and communism. Now Iranian women affirmed they too were independent and refused to be co-opted.

Similar demonstrations were held in many cities across Iran: from the industrial Isfahan in the centre, Urumiyah, Kermanshah and Sanandaj in the west and Bandar Abbas, the main port on the Persian Gulf in the south.

As the Islamists laid the foundations for their new authoritarian state, nothing shook their confidence more than women on the streets fighting for their rights. Their response was swift. Around two hundred Islamists, almost entirely consisting of men, surrounded the women protesters in Tehran with slogans like 'We follow the Quran, we don't want women without Hijab', 'Foreign doll, get lost', 'Neither Eastern, nor Western, only the Islamic Republic.' Not content with merely verbal abuse, some threw stones at women. Some tried to beat them up.

Most alarmingly, some of the Islamist thugs were armed and shot their rifles in the air. Women's slogans radicalised in response. 'Death to reaction,' some shouted. 'Freedom, Freedom, Death to Tyranny,' others went. There were even a few chants that targeted the man at the top: 'Death to Khomeini.'

A delegation made it to the prime minister's office. But the liberal-leaning and Muslim modernist prime minister, Mehdi Bazargan, was not in Tehran. He had gone to Qom for consultations with Khomeini. The women delegation instead met with Deputy Prime Minister Abbas Amirentezam. The delegation formally asked the government 'not to let the Iranian women return to the medieval age'.[16]

As the demonstrations wound up, many went back to the University of Tehran's campus for evening events commemorating the International Women's Day. They also made arrangements for the next big demonstration: 'See you Saturday in front of the Justice Ministry.'

* * *

The Hezbollahi mobs who attacked the demonstrators were, at that point in time, an apparent political minority. The interim government was led by liberal and left-leaning parties and the country's political scene seemed to be dominated by various leftists and left-leaning organisations. But if only the thugs hurled sticks and stones at women, it remained the case that most major political forces refused to support them. Apparently the Hijab was 'not a priority'. This refrain would be repeated time and time again in the decades to come.

Only small groups countered this prevailing attitude of total complacency. On 8 March, one political group that organised an event in the University of Tehran was the new Socialist Workers

Party of Iran, a small Trotskyist tendency whose founders had been activists in various Trotskyist groups in Europe and the US. One of their members, Kateh Vafadari, was a leading organiser of the 8 March demonstrations.[17]

But these Trotskyists were the exception that proved the rule. Even if many men from leftist groups had defended women marchers against regime supporters on 8 March, most of these groups were adamant that Hijab wasn't an issue worthy of the fight. Television, now controlled by pro-Khomeini revolutionaries, didn't air a single report about tens of thousands of women who had demonstrated for their rights.

For days on end, Kateh and her comrades travelled around, visiting both well-known intellectuals and ordinary women, trying to gain support for their cause. 'After years of repression, women didn't know about their rights,' she remembers. 'People didn't even knew there *was* an International Women's Day.' Among the people Kateh met was the celebrated communist poet, Siavash Kasraei. While he was generally approving, it was clear that his party, the Tudeh, wouldn't come to the support of the women.

The attitude on the 'progressive' Left was perhaps best exemplified by Homa Nateq, a French-educated historian then teaching at the University of Tehran and who sympathised with the Marxist New Left. In response to the events of March 1979, she made her position clear. Speaking in an interview, and appearing without the Hijab, she said: 'Our women are used to the Hijab. It has never been a problem for us. If in order to get our independence and freedom, we have to wear the Hijab, all women of Iran will do so willingly; if this is the price we have to pay to get rid of imperialism.' When Mehrangiz Kar, a young feminist lawyer, went to see Nateq to ask for her help in organising women, she wasn't allowed to see the esteemed historian. 'I have nothing to do with Savakis like you,' Nateq told her, bizarrely accusing her of collaborating with the former regime's secret police.[18] Faced with the 8 March protesters, Nateq likened them to the women who had come out against the socialist government of Salvador Allende in Chile in the 1970s, leading to the US-backed coup of 1973.

But the movement wasn't so easily deterred. One day after, on 9 March, thousands of women protested in front of the University of Tehran. The gates had been locked. Hezbollahi mobs attacked the women with snowballs stuffed with stones.

On 10 March, the planned march in front of the Ministry of Justice was disrupted by shots in the air. It included at least ten thousand marchers. They were women from all parts of Tehran. Employees of the state broadcaster had a prominent delegation. Under Qotbzadeh, they had been amongst the first who were forced to cover up.

The shots in the air didn't disperse the women, even though at least one woman lost consciousness and a pregnant woman had a seizure. A group of mostly male students formed a chain of support around the protesters as some of them entered the Ministry of Justice. Many had different forms of veil on: some with long black chadors, some with small scarves. They were united in their defence of freedom.

As women entered the ministry's courtyard, they shouted 'Compulsory Hijab will be a shroud for burying freedom'. Leading the delegation was Mother Sepehri. Three of her sons had been killed as members of a Marxist guerrilla group fighting the Shah's regime. How could anyone accuse her of being against the revolution? Alongside her, Parivash Khajehnoori, a member of the Iranian Bar Association, read out a statement by female lawyers.[19]

This time the state broadcaster couldn't ignore the protesters. It attacked them as 'leading people's minds to deviation and supporting the previous regime'. The Organisation of People's Fadai Guerrillas, the same organisation which counted the three martyred sons of Mother Sepehri as supporters, published a statement that managed to ignore the central demands of protesters, i.e. opposition to the compulsory Hijab. Still the organisation did attack the Hezbollahis as 'counter-revolutionary reactionaries who, whether they know it or not, were instruments of imperialism and domestic reaction'.

Although it has often gone unacknowledged, the women's daily marches weren't in vain and managed to gain a concession. On 11 March, Mahmud Taleqani, a popular Tehrani cleric and the nominal head of the Revolutionary Council, gave an interview to *Kayhan* which promised that Hijab wasn't meant to be compulsory. He still defended Khomeini as a 'father who was giving advice to his children' and 'pleaded' with women to 'dress modestly'.[20] So it appeared that forcing compulsory Hijab was off the agenda for the moment. This created a rift in the movement as some women believed that the protests should stop now.

On 18 March, *Kayhan* made the case. In an editorial it said: 'We should say right here, honestly and loudly: If women's demonstrations were correct until yesterday, from today and in the current conditions, they are wrong and to continue them illogically is to commit treason. Yes, treason!'

Many prominent woman intellectuals agreed. Daneshvar said: 'We should first take care of the economy, get our agriculture to some level, bring about a government of justice and freedom... and we can then get to side issues...such as woman's attire.'

This attitude soon infected sections of the international feminist movement. When the United Nations held its International Women's Conference in Copenhagen in July 1980, the walls were plastered with photographs, not of Iranian women who had come out with the message of global sisterhood a few months before, but of Khomeini, kindly provided by the Islamic Republic's delegates. Ironically, the conference had originally been planned to take place in Tehran but was moved because of the revolution.[21]

* * *

The regime's retreat had been temporary, a momentary pause that allowed it to gather its forces. As the Islamic Republic was formally declared in April 1979, it soon showed that it had no intention of allowing women to wear what they liked. In July 1980, just as the UN Women's Conference in Copenhagen was being inundated with posters of Khomeini, the Revolutionary

Council published an official statement which said: 'Women are not allowed to enter government offices without Islamic attire.' On 8 July, Ali Qoddosi, the prosecutor general, promised to prosecute women who were not observing the rule.[22]

Signs that announced the refusal of services to non-Hijabi women had started going up across the country. In Ramadan in 1981, the regime's judiciary declared these signs to be compulsory in a host of public places.[23] The government soon published detailed by-laws for civil servants that restricted clothing for men and women. Men were prohibited from wearing short sleeves and gold, seen as impermissible for men in the Islamic tradition. Women were asked to wear 'long cloaks with long sleeves that cover the wrist well and go below the knees', 'a scarf that covers the hair entirely', 'simple and thick socks' and 'clothing with simple colours'. They were explicitly barred from wearing any make-up. The revolution had declared war on colour.

These strictures weren't simply enforced by declaration. Pro-Khomeini mobs attacked unveiled women in cities such as Tabriz, Hamedan and Kerman, threatening them with burning or throwing acid on their faces. In Hamedan, vigilante signs went up that said no women without the full chador were allowed on the streets.

Secure in his power, as he progressively eliminated his rivals, Khomeini gave increasingly aggressive speeches in which he exhorted men and women to end some of their most mundane pleasures: something as simple as men and women going to the beach together, which had long been the norm in coastal cities of the Caspian Sea in the north. After being informed that this was still going on, Khomeini gave a furious speech.

'Islam will stop all the pursuit of lust,' he thundered.[24] 'Islam won't let these people swim naked. We will peel their skin off! Women and men going naked to the sea and then naked women going to cities? People are Muslims and we will peel their skin off if this happens. This is the civilisation these people want. This is the freedom they speak about; the Western freedom... I know that the government is stopping this. If not, people will. Will the people of Mazandaran or Rasht allow their beaches to be like before? Will the people of Bandar Pahlavi [Anzali] allow women and men to go to the sea together and have fun?'

In 1983, the Iranian parliament, dominated by pro-Khomeini MPs, passed an Islamic penal code that brought about some of the strictest interpretation of Islamic rule in the modern era.[25] Not only did it criminalise any non-wearing of the Hijab, anywhere in public, it also legislated a severe punishment for it: seventy-four blows of the lash. Millions of Iranian women were now being threatened with being lashed for doing what they had been doing for decades: not covering their hair.

Those who had ridiculed the anti-Hijab protests of 8 March 1979 soon came to understand their mistake. The same thugs who had attacked women were emboldened by Khomeini to attack and kill all their political opponents on the street. Within a matter of years, all non-Khomeinist forces, whether Islamist or secular, whether left-wing or right-wing, were suppressed. Tens of thousands of their supporters were executed in the dark decade of the 1980s. Among the executed was Qotbzadeh, the same head of the state broadcaster who had forced women presenters to cover up after the revolution.

Saddam Hussein invaded Iran in September 1980 and an eight-year war ensued. At home, the repression only increased. Thousands of women who had burst into political life with the revolution now went through years of prison and torture. Many were executed. Some had done as little as selling a few dissident newspapers on the streets. All women judges were expelled.

Nateq, the female Marxist historian who had so vehemently opposed the women protesters, soon owned up to her own mistakes. Having fled to Britain to work for BBC's Persian-language service, she said: 'I was so wrong.' Speaking in 1984, she recounted her role in 1979. 'I was the one who disrupted the demonstrations and helped shut them down. I betrayed women. I called them counter-revolutionaries and liberals that should be opposed. I said Hijab didn't matter. What I didn't understand was that someone who tells you what to wear will soon also tell you what to think.'[26]

By then it was too late.

* * *

The Islamic dress code was enforced by many armed groups of men who patrolled the streets of cities and towns around the country. The Islamic Revolution Committees had been founded by the order of Khomeini, the very day after the revolution.

Supplanting the regular police force and the newly founded Islamic Revolutionary Guards Corps, the committees focused on the petty task of harassing everyday Iranians for their basic lifestyle choices. Some were particularly brutal. If a woman was found with a scarf that had slid down her hair, the guards used a drawing pin to attach it until her forehead bled. Men found with short-sleeves sometimes had their hands dipped in white dye. Not respecting any legal norms or due process, the committees could enter a home and seize whatever they didn't like. Something as simple as owning a VCR could lead to jail and blows of the lash.

Ahmad Shamlu, perhaps the greatest Persian-language poet of his generation, wrote some of his most memorable verses in this era.

> They smell your mouth,
> To see if you said 'I love you.'
> They smell your heart.
> Darling, these are strange times.
> They arrest love on the streets...
> There are butchers
> Waiting on every street corner,
> Blood dripping from their cleavers.

Women may have lost many battles, but they never surrendered in the war. Even as compulsory Hijab was enforced, women pressed their demands and their fight for equality. Taleqani's daughter and comrade-in-arms, Azam, always kept to her strict Hijab. But this didn't stop her from incessantly running for president, defying the dominant interpretation of the constitution that barred women from running.[27] Over the years new generations of Iranian feminists came to agitate and organise for a variety of rights. Many considered the compulsory Hijab to be a lost cause and they focused on other terrains of struggle.

Women also resisted in more subtle ways. In the late 1990s and 2000s, the scarves started growing shorter and more colourful. The long cloaks became tighter. Trousers were replaced with tights. Make-up made a comeback. The regime retaliated to these incursions on its authority. Something as simple as a lipstick that was too red could land a woman in jail or under the blows of the lash. The mere act of wearing tights so inflamed pro-regime voices that hundreds of articles and hours of parliamentary debate were devoted to stopping it. But with dogged persistence, women kept up. They never gave up. They never submitted.

And if compulsory Hijab had gone off the main feminist agenda in favour of loftier goals, it soon made a comeback. By 2012, when the Liberal Students and Alumni Association organised a social media campaign and asked people to post their pictures with the slogan 'No to Compulsory Hijab', thousands answered the call including many prominent Iranians, men and women, veiled or unveiled.[28] Among them was Mehrangiz Kar, that young lawyer who had been thrown out of Homa Nateq's office in 1979 and who had dedicated decades of her life to advocacy for women's rights.

Another supporter of the campaign was a feisty thirty-six-year-old journalist named Masih Alinejad. A parliamentary reporter who had been kicked out when she broke a story about massive bonuses paid to MPs, Alinejad had been forced to leave Iran like many other journalists of her generation. In London and then New York City, she emerged as a loud activist, known for her unapologetic persistence, pursuit of regime officials (be it by phone or by following them on streets during their foreign trips) and, eventually, for her phenomenally curly hair. No one would guess from her later appearance that she had been brought up by strictly devout parents in a village in Mazandaran, the kind of observant Muslims who formed Khomeini's main support base.

One day, in May 2014, she was scrolling through old photos when she saw a picture of herself, from her days in Tehran, that caught her attention. It showed her driving, but without her Hijab. She thought of many moments like this; little moments of courage when women dared to do something small that could cost them big time: a ride or a walk without the perennial scarf, a secret kiss in the corner of a park. She called this a moment of *Azaadi-haaye Yavashaki* which was translated to English in the inelegant formulation 'Stealthy Freedoms'. A better translation would have been 'secret freedoms'. But the English translation didn't matter since this was a message intended for her fellow Iranian women. And they answered in unbelievable, unprecedented numbers.

The Facebook page Masih had built soon received thousands of pictures and videos sent by women who wanted to flaunt their disregard for the rules of the Islamic Republic. Some blurred their faces but many didn't, displaying awe-inspiring courage. They showed themselves driving without Hijab, as Masih had done. They showed themselves in cable cars in the snowy hills of northern Tehran, without the Hijab. They showed themselves smoking a hookah in a traditional Iranian restaurant, without the Hijab, breaking two rules at once. They showed themselves singing and dancing by the sea or in a forest. They showed themselves biking on a path far from the prying eyes of the pro-regime bruisers. In short, they showed themselves living as women, their daily routines a crime. The Stealthy Freedoms Facebook page soon found hundreds of thousands of members. Today it has more than one million.[29]

The response of the regime was swift and brutal. Thirty-five years after the Islamist goons had beaten up feminists protesting compulsory Hijab, the now well-established Islamic Republic showed that it had as little tolerance as ever.

A mere week after the page had opened, Tehran's Friday prayer leader, Kazem Sediqqi, used one of the most important pulpits of the Islamic Republic to tackle the issue. 'In some areas of cities, scarves are taken off and people don't observe any Hijab,' he said. 'Satellite channels and the internet are promoting all sorts of non-Hijab-wearing.'

A well-known anchor of the state TV, Vahid Yaminpoor, had a more thuggish response. On his Google Plus page, Yaminpoor attacked Masih and likened her to 'whores who are not young anymore and hold no sexual attraction so they now deceive the younger women into their business.'[30]

Masih kept up her fight, attracting the kind of audiences that most activists can only dream of. In 2017, she launched the White Wednesdays campaign, asking women to wear white scarves on Wednesdays as a protest against the regime. Once more, thousands answered her call. In many ways, she proved to be the most influential anti-regime activist in a generation. She had surprised not just the regime but many seasoned activists. Who knew that a fast-talking Mazandarani woman could provoke such fear in a regime that insisted on its own impregnable strength?[31]

But she was no longer alone. The movement had steeled Iranian women's fortitude and it would never be held back again. No other country in the world dared to impose a dress code on every woman by brute force. How could Iran?

On 27 December 2017, a young woman climbed onto a box on Tehran's busy Enqelab Avenue (named *enqelab* in honour of the Islamic Revolution). The thirty-two-year-old Vida Movaheddi took her scarf off and tied it to a stick. The white scarf fluttered in the air, attracting the attention of thousands of passers-by. Videos of the act soon went viral all around the world. Many women were quick to follow her. They became known as the Girls of Enqelab Avenue. By their act of protest, Vida and her comrades were reclaiming not just the street but the revolution. It was clear for anyone with eyes to see: they were making their own revolution.

Vida and the other Girls of Enqelab Avenue, at least thirty-five of them, were thrown into prison. Supreme Leader Khamenei picked 8 March 2018, International Women's Day (IWD), to condemn the women as 'deceived' and 'pathetic'.[32]

'They went through all that cost, thinking and propaganda just to deceive a few girls who would take their scarfs off? All their efforts led to this small and pathetic result,' Khamenei said. On the same day, the police arrested women who were trying to organise a gathering for IWD in front of the Ministry of Labour.[33]

Khamenei's tough talk only revealed his insecurity. While dozens of women had been thrown into prison just because they took their Hijab off, the Iranian judiciary issued an official interpretation of the Islamic Penal Code that targeted those who sent videos and pictures to Masih. In 2019, Mosa Qazanfarabadi, the head of Tehran's Revolutionary Court, specifically mentioned Masih and said those 'sending her videos without Hijab, from themselves or others, can be sentenced to one to ten years in prison'.[34]

But threats by the Supreme Leader and dozens of prosecution cases couldn't stop women who, like their mothers and grand-mothers, had never truly accepted an unjust imposition. Their daily resistance against the enforced Hijab never ceased. Now and then, they'd burst into the full glare of the media spotlight. In July 2022, a video went viral of Sepideh Rashno, a twenty-eight-year-old novelist who was attacked by a pro-regime woman on a busy bus in Tehran. The assailant, Rayehe Rabiee, had cautioned Sepideh for her 'bad Hijab'. When Sepideh disobeyed, Rayehe bit her on the hand. The regime, as expected, went on to arrest someone – not Rayehe, who had physically assaulted a passenger in public, but Sepideh.[35]

For every case that went viral online, thousands of others never made it to the news. In coffee shops, parks and streets, from Sareyn to Dezful and from Zahedan to Mashhad, these seemingly tiny acts of quotidian female resistance continued. They were met with repression by the regime but also ridicule or simple disregard by many professional Iran watchers and intellectuals. Meanwhile, in page after page of analysis about Iran and its fate, there was much talk of the nuclear programme, Khamenei's understanding of 'strategic depth' and the jockeying between various power factions inside the regime. What many missed was that these simple acts of female resistance amounted to what sociologist Assef Bayat had long ago termed 'Life as Politics'.[36] In other words, people's persistent desire to live out their basic rights had a profound political significance that went over the heads of those who were laser-focused on elite jockeying.

The Iranian women of 1979 had not been able to impose their rights on the nascent regime – despite their best efforts. But generations of Iranian women refused, at times quietly and at times boldly, to be remade in the regime's image. Whatever happens in Iran now, they cleared the path for the regime's demise.

In September 2022, many decades of daily resistance at last bore fruit. Women's rights were no longer the sideshow to the 'real' revolution. Women were the revolution.

Two

Yes, I Am a Woman: The Fight for Women's Rights

On 8 March 2023, International Women's Day was once more celebrated across the world. And so it was in Tehran. Here too prominent women's rights activists got up and spoke about their struggle to win equality. But they weren't speaking in packed halls or rarefied lecture theatres. They spoke in a prison.

For many in the Western world, the International Women's Day has long become a regular fixture on the calendar, marked by solemn promises and perfunctory declarations by this or that cabinet minister. The day's socialist origins have been erased; the corporate world now cashes in. The LA-based brand Birdy Grey offered discounts on its bridesmaid dresses and pyjamas and Nike featured women's running shoes and sport bras. Amazon suggested customers ask, 'Alexa, tell me about an incredible woman.' Even in countries such as India with militant feminist organisations with tens of millions of members, commerce is taking over. As Indian feminist Nilanjana Bhowmick wrote on 8 March 2023: 'We don't need discount vouchers for International Women's Day. We need equal rights.'[1]

But in Iran, celebrating International Women's Day remains a revolutionary act – and an illegal one. It's no surprise that women marked it behind bars.

As the regime cracked down on the revolt of Iranians in 2022 and 2023, it imprisoned more than 22,000 people by its own count. Many headed to Tehran's notorious Evin prison, joining activists who had already spent years behind the bars. For seasoned feminist activists in Evin, the Women, Life, Freedom movement vindicated their resistance to the regime when it was a lonelier battle. Now the fight for freedom was being waged by millions.

These activists were used to speaking in public rallies and to the media. Now they spoke in a small room in a prison far from reporters and TV cameras. Even the very fact of the meeting was kept completely confidential. Its details were only published ten days later.[2]

The list of speakers testifies to the exceptional nature of the Iranian feminist movement. Boasting decades of experience between them, they hailed from different generations and frequently from wildly different political backgrounds. But they achieved what the male opposition to the regime could not: uniting over shared goals.

There was Narges Mohammadi, fifty, a human rights activist who had spent most of the past couple of decades in jail and had been recently nominated for the Nobel Peace Prize. There was Bahare Hedayat, forty-one, a former student activist who had once supported working with reformist regime politicians before endorsing a more radical way forward. There was Fariba Kamal-Abadi, sixty-one, an educator who belonged to the Bahá'í faith, Iran's largest non-Muslim minority and one of its most oppressed communities. There was Golrokh Iraee, forty-three, being punished for an unpublished manuscript found in her home. There was Sepideh Qolian, twenty-eight, a workers' activist who had been arrested due to her tireless advocacy for sugarcane workers of southwestern Iran.

Golrokh was among the first to speak. In and out of prison since autumn 2016, she had been sentenced to six years for a host of activities such as campaigning to abolish capital punishment, publishing pictures without Hijab on her Facebook and sending reports on human rights violations to the United Nations. But all this paled compared to her most egregious crime: penning a short story. The story portrays a protagonist who is enraged after watching the Iranian-American film *The Stoning of Soraya M.*, starring the Oscar-winning Shohre Aghdashloo, and goes on to burn the pages of the Qur'an in protest. Golrokh had not published this story; the Revolutionary Guards found it in a house search. For this 'crime' alone, she earned five years in prison. Meanwhile her husband, Arash Sadeghi, languished in a separate prison, denied chemotherapy for his bone cancer. None of this daunted Golrokh as she addressed her comrades.

'The most important characteristic of the recent protests is their crushing of corrupt structures of customs and traditions whose destructive mark has long been left on our bodies and minds,' she said. She could hardly hide her joy at the movement now on the march through all of Iran.

'The young generation's anger from the murder of Mahsa turned into an uprising which aims to overthrow the regime,' she continued. 'It has targeted the whole regime. Its progressive slogans have crushed structures based on sexism... An important page of history has turned in the recent revolutionary movement. The foundations that hold up tyranny and domination have been crushed.'

The next speaker, Fariba, struck a different tone to Golrokh, the revolutionary firebrand. Like other devout Baháʼís, she was barred from partisan activity by her faith but had spent most of the past twenty years incarcerated solely due to her role as an organiser of Baháʼí affairs in Iran. Fariba had been barred from university education as she belonged to a religion not officially recognised by the regime. Yet she had studied in the clandestine Baháʼí Institute for Higher Education (BIHE), founded in 1989. This institute's classes took place in believers' living rooms to avoid detection. She had written a BA thesis about the Baháʼí faith and transcendental philosophy and an MA thesis on educational psychology. She had then gone on to teach in BIHE.

What united Golrokh and Fariba was an ardent belief in gender equality, one that had been shared by the founders of the Bahá'í faith.

'I want to speak on the concept of unity today,' Fariba said. 'We must learn to see humans first, before seeing women or men. I believe that the recent movement showed attention to unity. The people of Iran showed that they've gone beyond differences based on ethnicity, gender and the like. This speaks to their maturity. But it should be noted that it is women who are at the forefront of the movement.'

With nine years between them, Narges and Bahare bookended a generation defining their politics around support for the *Eslahtalabs* or 'demanders of reform', a faction of the regime that had, often half-heartedly, embraced the need for democratic change in the late 1990s and early 2000s. The faction emerged in the aftermath of the 1997 presidential elections, won by Mohammad Khatami, a cleric and former culture minister known for his mild manners and chocolate-coloured robes. The elections were not free or fair by any means but, for the first time since 1980, they were competitive – if still limited to candidates within the regime. Millions had voted for Khatami in the hope that he could help democratise the regime and propel Iran as a latecomer to the Third Wave of global democratisation. A period of ferocious struggle began: Iranians suddenly had groundbreaking freedom of speech, association and assembly. They could write and read books and newspapers that would have never been allowed before. They could gather in mass meetings on university campuses to raise democratic demands. But the regime's core establishment, led by Supreme Leader Khamenei, fought back and ultimately managed to snuff out the reform movement and its partisans.

When Khatami was elected, Narges was twenty-five and Bahare only sixteen. They both came of age during the Reform Era and its aftermath. They had both endorsed candidates in many presidential and parliamentary elections. They had both served on the leadership of Tahkim Vahdat, an originally Islamist student union that had come to be a reformist bastion during the Khatami era. Most importantly, they had used the few freedoms granted to organise for women's rights and democracy. They were rewarded for their efforts with repeated arrests, torture and decades in prison. In 2023, they stood in full solidarity with the movement on the streets and committed to getting rid of the regime they had initially tried to reform from within.

'People have come to believe that their survival is in contradiction with the survival of the regime,' Bahare said. 'The movement for Women, Life, Freedom has now given us positive slogans. Previously, we had negative slogans against the regime but we didn't have a slogan that could have general acceptance. Now we have hopeful slogans. This movement is not divided. It paints a future defined by the slogans that seek the overthrow of the regime.'

Using her status as one of Iran's best-known political prisoners, Narges Mohammadi had published an open message, calling on supporters of the movement to 'conquer the streets with pro-women symbols on International Women's Day'. Now at the Evin event, she spoke with a cool authority stemming from decades of activism.

'I strongly believe that the people's will now demands an end to the Islamic Republic,' she said. 'They want an end to a system that has brought our society to the point of collapse. We want a system that could bring about freedom, equality and democracy.'

The movement for Women, Life, Freedom was a 'revolutionary movement' that made clear the need for 'transitioning away from the Islamic Republic and toward democracy'. She explained further, 'Women have a very decisive role in this transition.'

Narges addressed the Iranian youth: 'I call on the girls and boys of my country! With passion, joy, love and faith in victory and with respect for each other's ideas and beliefs, with the aim of creating empathy and solidarity; form "Girls of Neighbourhoods" groups in all your neighbourhoods! Support each other.'

The next generation didn't need to be told twice. Next to Narges, waiting to speak, was Sepideh Qolian, who had been sentenced to almost twenty years in prison. She began by declaring herself 'an activist from the margins'. Hailing from the city of Dezful in the southwestern province of Khuzestan, she had been repeatedly harassed, beaten up and arrested because of her sympathetic coverage of the Haft-Tappeh Sugarcane Workers Trade Union as a journalist. She recalled when 'Women, Life, Freedom' was a 'slogan from the margins', unheard of by most in the country. Now it was chanted by millions.

41

'This movement showed that margins and the centre have joined up with one another,' Sepideh said. 'I believe the movement will surely continue.'

As she said these words, Sepideh escalated her ambitions. She pointed to the Persian rollets (a cream roulade) she had baked for her cellmates that day and said: 'After our victory, I will go to Ahvaz's Clock Square and I will bake these rollets for millions of Iranians!'

Sepideh was released on bail a few days after this speech. Right outside prison, she jumped up and down and chanted against Khamenei, using a popular slogan that compared the grand dictator to Zahhak, a legendary tyrant in Iranian folklore, who murdered children to feed their brains to his snakes. She then joined her family and headed to her beloved Khuzestan. They had barely gotten on the road when the car was stopped by security forces. The guards beat her up and arrested her again, effectively abducting her from her family's car.

Her words in that clandestine gathering, as well as those of her sisters, soon made their way out of Evin and were widely disseminated. It turned out that there had been smaller International Women's Day gatherings in other prisons around the country, including Qarchak prison, not far from Evin, notorious for overflowing sewage, dirty drinking water and cells designed for cows, not humans. Behind bars, and in claustrophobic cells, Iranian women had commemorated their international day; standing together across various faiths, generations and political affiliations.

Impressive as each of them were, together these women represented more than the sum of their parts; they were the faces of a decades-long effort to revive women's rights activity in Iran; an effort that started in the late 1990s and, despite gruesome repression, had not only survived but matured politically. Now it was poised to take the lead in Iranian society.

* * *

In early 1998, Iran was going through a momentous political battle and nothing reflected this better than the newspapers. President Khatami, still in his first few months in office, had allowed for unprecedented freedom of the press. But the judiciary didn't agree. As a result, hundreds of thousands of Iranians bought pro-reformist newspapers every day, while the judiciary was on the lookout for any that crossed red lines, eager to prosecute and shut them down.

The headlines of Tehran's daily *Hamshahri* on 28 February 1998 illustrated tensions approaching fever pitch. In a speech, Khatami promised that 'in civil society, people determine things, not the government'. Ayatollah Yazdi, head of the judiciary, asked the newspapers to stop criticising the judiciary. But while student union elections were being hotly contested and a protest rally was held in front of the University of Tehran on that day, the most momentous (and brief) news item could easily have been missed: 'On 11 March, Tehran will host an exhibition of female book publishers.'

On first glance, the exhibition was a small affair. Forty-six women who ran publishing houses or women's journals gathered in a small hall to show their latest titles. They were joined by women who were active in NGOs dedicated to children's rights or the environment, forming a tiny space of civic activity that the regime hadn't encroached upon yet. But a page had been turned in the history of women's activism. Exactly nineteen years after the 8 March demonstrations of 1979, Iranian women had come together to launch a new era of feminist activity. The book exhibition, attended by thousands of interested women, helped make contacts and gave new visibility to a group of activists who, despite their widely varying backgrounds, had come to unite for the cause of women. While women's magazines and publishing houses acted like virtual organisers for feminists, women-owned bookstores became physical spaces that emerged as a new public square.

Female publishers thus came to constitute an unlikely group of pioneering rebels. Leading the pack was Shahla Lahiji who had, in 1983, founded one of the first-ever female-led publication houses in Iran, *Roshangaran* or 'the Enlighteners'. Born in 1942 in Tehran, she was a bit older than the average activist but this brought her experience and authority. With her endless energy and can-do attitude, she was exactly the type of person that an emerging, progressive movement needed. A veteran who had written for the press and radio since the age of sixteen, Shahla had struggled to keep working after 1979, faced with the regime's hostility. In the 1980s, as wartime Iran experienced a suffocating cultural era, she worked hard to keep independent publishing alive. She published pioneering books on women's history and women's studies. On her list she could boast both women such as the activist Mehrangiz Kar and men such as the celebrated historian Fereydon Adamiat. She published plays and screenplays by Bahram Beizaei, the doyen of Iran's theatre and cinema who had been mostly barred from work after the revolution. In short, she had been a one-woman bulwark of intellectual and cultural resistance. Now leading the Society of Women Publishers, she used her years of experience to help usher in a new stage in the feminist struggle.

Women's demands were now in the spotlight. As before, many men insisted to these women that their demands were not a priority. But once again women would not listen. This time around, they doggedly held their events, formed their own groups and pursued their demands.

* * *

On 8 March 1999, a year after the book exhibition, International Women's Day was publicly commemorated for the first time since the establishment of the Islamic Republic of Iran in April 1979. The event was organised by a number of women publishers as well as women who had been organising book clubs. In the past two decades, Islamist women activists had organised a variety of events. But for the first time, Iranian secular feminists were now in the lead; although they often worked closely with those from a devout or even Islamist background. On that day, plans were announced for the foundation of the Cultural Centre for Women (CCW), the first women-focused, non-religious organisation in decades.

By describing itself as 'cultural', the CCW hoped to evade suppression by the regime. At the very least, its name sounded reassuringly unpolitical. In reality, this was an organisation intent on campaigning for women's rights and it had no intention of retreating from the political battlefield.

This was evident if you took a look at the young woman who was perhaps the most iconic co-founder of the CCW. The thirty-year-old Nooshin Ahmadi Khorasani had an infectious laugh that could make her comrades forget the tough odds they often faced. Holding a MA in Women's Studies from the University of Tehran, Khorasani had run a left-leaning publishing house with her husband. Among their most popular publications was a literary journal called *The Second Sex*, named after the 1949 book by the French philosopher Simone de Beauvoir, which would soon become a must-read for a new generation of feminists. She was both widely well-read and tactically ingenious and soon proved invaluable to the movement. This wave of feminists was not in search of personality cults, and Nooshin was one of many women who would debate with each other for hours on questions like the relationship between Marxism and feminism and a variety of tactics. But they also knew how to come together when engaged in common struggle: against both the regime and the patriarchy that permeated their society.

As the Iranian reformists fought to open up the political space, they called their strategy 'pressure from below, bargaining on the top'. The nascent feminist movement adopted a similar strategy. It pursued independent and grassroots tactics and campaigns while it maintained a tacit alliance with women in official politics, including those serving inside the Khatami administration, to push for its goals. When parliamentary elections were held in February 2000, despite the usual restrictions that limited eligible candidates to factions inside the regime, pro-Khatami reformists gained a solid majority. The new parliament included thirteen women MPs who were almost all reformists.

The new generation of reformist women MPs brought an immediate change of culture to the new parliament. While they were still bound by the compulsory Hijab, they mostly ditched the long chador in favour of less strict clothing. They desegregated the parliamentary quarters and insisted on equality with their male colleagues. Most importantly, they worked closely with the feminist movement, including secular feminists, to advocate for women's issues. During their four-year mandate, they passed more than thirty bills to further women's rights. While the regime's Guardian Council, a body of clerics and jurists appointed by the Supreme Leader, threw out most of these, many, such as banning child marriage and increasing the rights of women in divorce and custody matters, stuck.

One of the most striking new female MPs was the thirty-one-year-old Fatemeh Haghighatjoo. Born in a humble family in southern Tehran, Haghighatjoo had been a student activist and was now among the youngest reformist MPs. In a parliament dominated by powerful men, who expected a young woman with little political experience to achieve anything? But she soon proved a force to be reckoned with. In the early days of the parliament, Fatemeh got together with some of her fellow female MPs to demand the appointment of female cabinet ministers, something that Iran hadn't had since 1979. The leading lights of the reformist faction in the parliament didn't take the demand seriously and brushed it off as unimportant. But they were shocked when Fatemeh and her colleagues threatened to withhold their votes on key issues. When Fatemeh's parliamentary tactics led to reformist Nasrollah Jahangard failing to get a vote of confidence as Khatami's communications minister, the reformist leaders started listening. A compromise was reached when Khatami appointed a woman, Ashraf Borujerdi, as deputy interior minister, a position that was hardly less important than a cabinet minister.[3]

But the most significant campaign of feminists pursuing their aims in civil society in conjunction with the Khatami administration came around a shared demand: for Iran to accede to the Convention on the Elimination of All Forms of Discrimination Against Women (CEDAW). This treaty had been adopted by the United Nations General Assembly in 1979 and had since been signed and ratified by the vast majority of countries in the world. In September 2000, even Saudi Arabia ratified the treaty.

While Khatami, like all other previous presidents of the Islamic Republic, had failed to appoint a woman as cabinet minister, he *had* launched the Centre for Women's Participation as part of his presidential office and made sure that the new centre's head, activist Zahra Shojaee, would be present in all cabinet meetings. In 1999, Shojaee, who boasted a PhD in political science from the University of Tehran, declared that joining CEDAW was a goal of the administration.

Since it codified a wide variety of women's rights, CEDAW proved to be a perfect platform for bringing together feminists from diverse backgrounds. The fact that it had been accepted by the vast majority of UN member states meant that it could hardly be painted as some radical document. Adoption of its measures would amount to a legal revolution in Iran since it enshrines gender equality in law, requires states to take positive measures to end discrimination and provides for women's right to work, which it regards as 'an inalienable right of all human beings', as well as equal pay for equal work.

The fight for CEDAW was waged both on the streets and in the halls of power, by both secular and Islamic feminists. In women's meetings, now multiplying in cultural centres and universities around the country, different provisions of the treaty were read out loud. Feminist lawyers and jurists devised legal strategies against discriminatory laws, hoping that the adoption of CEDAW would help strike them down. In 2001, the Khatami administration sponsored a bill of accession to CEDAW and sent it to the parliament. The bill slowly made its way through the parliament and it was finally ratified (with some reservations) in 2003.

49

The establishment was quick to fight back. The Guardian Council nullified the CEDAW accession bill and it went to the Expediency Council, a body (also entirely appointed by the Supreme Leader) that was meant to conciliate between the parliament and the Guardian Council. But the council, headed by veteran regime founder and ex-president Akbar Hashemi Rafsanjani, refused to take any action on what was now considered a red button issue. CEDAW accession withered on the vine.[4]

Akbar's daughter, Faeze Hashemi, had been a pioneering female MP and women's activist in the pre-reform days. In 1998, she had started the newspaper *Zan* (Women), the first daily dedicated to women since the revolution. Like the pro-reformist press of the time, it was soon shut down. It was accused of criticising the compulsory Hijab, supporting feminism and publishing a news piece about Farah Pahlavi, the former queen of Iran, when even mentioning her was illegal. It had particularly incensed the judiciary by running a cartoon that mocked the fact that, in Islamist-based Iranian law, a woman was worth half a man in blood money matters, one of many laws that would have been challenged by adoption of CEDAW. Years later, Faeze went to Britain to study. She wrote her MA thesis at Birmingham City University on CEDAW and she argued that nothing in the treaty contradicted Islam.[5]

* * *

In 2003, just as CEDAW was being debated in the halls of power, a new milestone took place in Iranian commemorations of the

International Women's Day. In the past few years, the day had been marked by events in bookshops and cultural centres. But the women's movement was now able to get a permit to organise a public rally on the day in Tehran's iconic Laleh Park. Not long ago, feminists symbols such as IWD could only be whispered about. Now they would take the public spotlight. Violence against women was picked as a central theme of the event. As the United States was preparing its invasion of Iraq, peace became another theme. At least seven hundred people, mostly women, assembled surrounded by a heavy police presence which insisted on segregating men from women.

Nooshin Ahmadi Khorasani, who now also ran the website Feminist School, started her speech by condemning the Iraq War.[6]

She continued 'How can we congratulate each other on International Women's Day when the policies of the World Bank are being implemented in this country, and we know women to be the first victims of this structural adjustments?' She asked, 'How can we congratulate each other when women do two-thirds of all the labour in the world but only get 5% of all incomes? How can we be happy when a nine-year-old girl is married off with the permission of her father?'

She was followed by the scholar Firouzeh Mohajer who also condemned the Iraq War and spoke of peace as a necessity for women all over the region: 'Peace for the Iraqi woman, peace for the Palestinian woman, peace for the Israeli woman.' Other speakers spoke about CEDAW and against Iran's misogynist laws. Among the most articulate was Shirin Ebadi, who became

Iran's first female judge at the age of twenty-three, but was barred from practising law after the establishment of the Islamic Republic. 'We women will get our social rights,' she promised.

But divisions in the movement were also becoming clear. Although the event had been supported by reformist MPs, some of the speakers showed their impatience with Khatami, who had been re-elected in 2001. Lawyer Shadi Sadr said if Iran was to join CEDAW with reservations, it was better not to join at all. Some of the female MPs present complained that activists failed to support them enough.

The disappointment of people like Sadr was not surprising. Almost six years into the Khatami administration, its lofty democratic goals had gone unreached. When met with the resistance of Khamenei and the regime establishment, Khatami and allies had refused to stand their ground.

But in autumn 2003, another important milestone came for the struggle of Iranian women. Shirin Ebadi was awarded the Nobel Peace Prize. 'For her efforts for democracy and human rights… especially the struggle for rights of women and children.'[7] She was the first Muslim woman to ever win the prize.

On her return from Oslo after accepting the award, Shirin Ebadi was received by at least thirty thousand Iranians who had gathered in Tehran's Mehrabad airport to welcome her to the country.[*]

---

[*] I was all of fifteen years old but I remember going to Mehrabad with my parents and their comrades. I covered that exciting night in my nascent blog. I distinctly remember passing Vice President Abtahi in a car and my father shouting at him: 'Why didn't you bring Khatami with you?

This was once more a moment of unity as activists were joined in the airport by Haghighatjoo and a number of other reformist MPs as well as Khatami's Vice President in Parliamentary Affairs Mohammad Ali Abtahi.

As Ebadi was arriving on an Air France flight from Paris, the symbolism couldn't be more obvious. Twenty-four years ago, millions had gathered to welcome Khomeini who had arrived at the same airport on the same flight. Thousands now had come to demand a renewal of the revolutionary spirit.

'This award doesn't belong to me,' Ebadi said as she spoke to the crowds. 'It belongs to all of you who work with passion in these difficult conditions. It belongs to all the people of Iran. It belongs to all those who work for human rights, peace and democracy in Iran.'[8]

Buoyed by the electrifying triumph, women's groups geared up for more activism. They prepared for a second public rally for International Women's Day in March 2004. A six-month campaign was to be launched on that day aimed at organising a mass petition to demand more legal protections for victims of violence against women.

But in the afternoon of 8 March 2004, as women started to gather for the historic event, they were told by the security forces that the interior ministry had annulled the permit at 11 a.m. that very morning. The Khatami administration had stabbed the movement in the back.[9] These were the days before smartphones; many had not heard the news before they got to the park's amphitheatre for the event that was supposed to start at 5 p.m. Guards turned them away, but a few brave women insisted on staying.

Ultimately, around forty women sat in the amphitheatre, surrounded by police forces who kettled them, not letting anyone enter or leave the gathering. Things got heated when a nineteen year-old woman trying to film the event was attacked by a plain-clothes officer. He destroyed the tape and injured her arm. But to the surprise of security forces, women kept arriving. Soon, there would be at least five hundred women who encircled the police forces. Many women had come with their husbands and small children. Police had tried to isolate the women but now they themselves were under siege.

Separated by a row of security forces, women started to do all that they could to join each other. They clapped and chanted slogans while marching in circles. The most common slogan of the day was: 'CEDAW must be ratified!'

They sang 'Oh Iran', an unofficial national anthem steeped in Iranian patriotism and which provides an alternative to the regime's dour official anthem. They sang 'My Schoolmate', a revolutionary song that promised solidarity against tyranny.

Despite all the difficulties, an activist was able to give a speech:

For centuries, they've taught women to be silent, to be subdued, to be a slave. But I am not a slave, I won't be subdued, I won't be silent. I won't be patient. I am a woman who revolts. I am a mother who is kind. But to defend my rights, I have a heart that is grand, claws that are sharp and, most importantly, a spirit full of passion. Yes, I am a woman, in battle with traditions. I defend my womanhood in its entirety.

As the women were on their way out, they were attacked by a swarm of cops. Hundreds of police forces, led by some senior officers, rained batons on the women as they searched for those who had given interviews to BBC and Deutsche Welle. An activist who had attended the gathering wrote an anonymous eyewitness report and lamented that none of the thousands of ordinary people in the park had come to help the women. 'Like thousands of other days, this day, too, will be forgotten,' she wrote.

Her pessimism spoke to the zeitgeist. With dozens of newspapers closed and hundreds of activists in jail, things seemed to have hit an impasse. 8 March 2003 had been celebrated as the first ever legal rally for International Women's Day in the history of the Islamic Republic. It also turned out to be the last. The authorities never issued a permit again.

* * *

But women did not lower their voice for a moment. The enthusiasm and zeal sparked by the movement could not be easily extinguished. At any given time, dozens of women-led campaigns were going on. Some protested misogynist programming by state TV. Some opposed crackdown on particular NGOs.

In the run-up to the presidential elections of 2005, women no longer contented themselves with simply supporting the reformist candidates Mostafa Moyin and Mehdi Karroubi. They now came with their own agenda.

On 1 June, Azam Taleqani helped organise a demonstration to protest the disqualification of all female candidates for presidency including Taleqani herself. It was attended by around a hundred people. But many were already losing hope in such tactics. On the very same day, a group of women decided to organise a rally in front of the University of Tehran to 'protest the discriminatory articles of the constitution'. This alienated many of the reformists. They had worked hard to stay within the system and had failed to make durable changes. They had long relied on some of the liberal-leaning provisions of the constitution, while ignoring the fact that the document gave the vast majority of power to the unelected and unaccountable Supreme Leader. Speaking of the need to alter the constitution itself meant going beyond the confines of the regime. Many were not prepared for that.

The event went ahead nonetheless. This time, the organisers didn't bother with the charade of asking for permission. On 17 June 2005, a few days before the elections, 6,000 assembled in front of the University of Tehran answering a call that had been issued by 90 groups and 350 activists. This was the largest women's rights gathering in Iran since 1979.[10] Similar events were held all over Iran by women's groups in East Azerbaijan, Kurdistan, Isfahan, Chaharmahal and Bakhtiari, Khorasan, Sistan and Balochistan, Luristan and Kermanshah provinces.

In Tehran, as police attacked the protesters, they now shouted back with slogans that went beyond particular demands. 'We are women, we are human, we are citizens of this land, we have no rights,' a series of chants went. 'Just laws and women's consciousness; that's the way to our emancipation.' Speakers openly called for a new referendum to change the constitution.

Reflecting on the event, Khorasani would later say: 'Yes, we women were able to experience a common and historical action without relying on political parties and organisations, and by only relying on our own force.'

Five days later, presidential elections were held and led to an enormous upset. The hard-line mayor of Tehran, Mahmoud Ahmadinejad, made it to the second round alongside the establishment figure Rafsanjani. With many of their supporters disillusioned and staying home, none of the reformist candidates made it to the second round. On 24 June, Ahmadinejad defeated Rafsanjani and became president.

If the Khatami administration had been non-cooperative, the new administration was positively hostile to women's rights and other civil society campaigns. Endorsed by Khamenei, the new government gave unparalleled power to the Islamic Revolutionary Guard Corps (IRGC) and started to drive back the mass movement that had mobilised for democratic demands in the reform era.

Women's activism persisted but they now faced exceptionally brutal suppression. In March 2006, efforts to hold an International Women's Day event in Tehran's Daneshju park were quashed with many injured following police attacks.[11] On 17 June, the anniversary of the previous rally, a new demonstration was organised, centred around a call for change in discriminatory laws on polygamy, divorce and custody. In a pioneering move,

workers' activists and spouses of some of the jailed trade union-
ists had also joined the rally. But when women gathered in
Tehran's Hafte Tir Square, they were met with hordes of police
officers who attacked them with batons and pepper spray; 70
people (42 women and 28 men) were arrested.[12]

With open forms of activity now severely restricted, women
took to more clandestine methods such as putting leaflets in mail-
boxes or giving them to people on the streets or in buses. In
August 2006, a historic new campaign was launched. The
Campaign for One Million Signatures was modelled on a
Moroccan campaign which had been launched on 8 March 1992,
gathering one million signatures to show public support for feminist reform of the country's family code. In 2004, the Moroccan
parliament had finally passed a new code that included more than
a hundred amendments asked for by the Moroccan feminists. The
Iranian campaign now aimed to organise its own mammoth petition that asked for changes in discriminatory laws in Iran.[13]

Gathering petition signatures had long been a staple of activist practice but what distinguished this campaign was its vast
grassroots and participatory model. Feminist activists went all
over the country to hold meetings that would educate interested
volunteers on discriminatory provisions in Iranian law. Activists
and volunteers would then be dispatched to the public, especially women, to explain their rights to them and agitate for
change. Few campaigns in history of Iranian politics had directly
involved so many people. In the first year, forty workshops were
held in Tehran which recruited five hundred volunteers as well

as events in a total of twelve cities. The authorities cracked down and fifty of the organisers were arrested. People's homes, where most events were held, were often raided. But the campaign had deep roots and it continued for years. In 2007, Ebadi would say: 'Now, even if we wanted to, we couldn't stop the One Million Signatures Campaign.'

But the campaign did come to an end, as did that era of feminist activity in Iran. In 2009, many regime critics put their differences aside and voted for Mirhossein Mousavi, a popular prime minister from the 1980s, as the main reformist candidate, hoping he could defeat Ahmadinejad and turn the tide. When Ahmadinejad was declared the winner, merely hours after the polls had closed, Mousavi opposed him and declared himself the real winner. Millions of Iranians came to streets in a months-long campaign that marked the most serious challenge to the Islamic Republic since 1979. Its crushing in blood, including dozens who were killed on the streets by security forces, was a turning point. Women's activism had to seek other avenues and strategies.

For Iranians who fought for democracy and equality, this period from 1997 to 2009 was ultimately an era of defeat. When it officially folded in 2013, the One Million campaign never declared how many signatures it had collected. It had failed to achieve most of its legislative demands. Iran never acceded to CEDAW. At the time of writing, it remains only one of the five countries in the world not to have signed the convention (alongside Somalia, Sudan, Tonga and the Vatican – the United States and Palau have signed the treaty but failed to ratify it).

Many other campaigns failed to achieve their goals. The campaign against stoning mobilised thousands in Iran and around the world. But this punishment, in which women convicted of adultery are stoned to death, remains on the books in Iran, and is still occasionally practised. The campaign to allow women into stadiums attracted much attention. But Iran today remains the only country in the world that bars women from attending most sports events.

It's wrong to view these defeats as setting Iranian women back. Yes, the whole road is, as Rosa Luxemburg put it, 'paved with nothing but thunderous defeats'. But the upsurge in feminist activism left indelible marks on Iranian society: it gave millions of women the courage and political ideals to *act*. This movement trained thousands of women activists who were to become crucial to the onward march of women's rights in Iran, and 8 March is now an unmissable date in the Iranian political calendar, even if it must be commemorated in prisons instead of parks. As women continue their struggle in Iran, they sometimes sing the Anthem for Equality which took shape spontaneously in the early 2000s. It best encapsulates the spirit of that era:[14]

> I will grow like a green shoot,
> I will overcome the wound on my body,
> Which I received just because I exist,
> I am a woman, a woman, a woman
> If we join voices,
> If we walk together,

If we take each other's hands,

We will be emancipated from tyranny,

We will build a new world,

A world of equality, empathy and sisterhood,

A better world, a happier world.

Three

We Want a Union! The Fight for the Labour Movement

As they walked off the job on 15 November 2022, the Isfahan steelworkers could hardly look more salt-of-the-earth working class. They marched as the chimneys hissed, dressed in their blue overalls and white helmets. Unlike protesters who had been shouting daring slogans all over Iran, targeting the top leaders of the regime, the marchers mostly remained silent, only sporadically chanting slogans such as 'Enough promises, our table is empty.' But their sombre march unsettled the regime more than many a spirited protest.

Founded in 1967 with help from the Soviet Union, the Isfahan Steel Company remains one of Iran's largest and most distinguished industrial corporations. Occupying massive grounds in central Iran, the state-owned company employs 16,000 people. Its rods, slabs and coils helped build Tehran's iconic Milad Tower and popular metro trains, Bushehr's nuclear refinery and the country's massive dams and expansive railways. The country ran on the labour of these workers. What if *they* joined the revolution? Courageous street actions and high school walkouts had inspired Iranians and the world. But serious strategists of both the regime and the opposition knew that strike action by the Iranian working class would escalate matters to another level. Everybody remembered that none other than the oil workers had administered the coup de grace on the Shah's regime in 1979. Now in 2022 as the movement continued fighting the regime forces in the streets and alleys, a new demand was on many lips: *etesaab-e-omoomi* – a general strike.

Striking workers exhilarated supporters of the revolution. As the steelworkers marched, passers-by and supporters filmed them, broadcasting their demonstration across social media.

The demands of the steelworkers might have seemed non-political to the uninitiated. They wanted an increase in wages, which were lower than other steel factories, and a reform in pay structures. But the timing of the strike was unmistakable; it coincided with the fourth anniversary of nationwide protests that had started with railing against fuel price hikes and ended in hundreds killed by security forces all over Iran. In fact, in order to derail the strike, the management had made a surprise payment of ten million rials (twenty-five pounds) to every worker. But they had walked off the job anyway.

Iran's labour activists left no doubt as to their support for the Women, Life, Freedom movement. Speaking to the London-based Iran International TV, Foad Keykhosravi, a leading figure of the Independent Iranian Workers Union (IIWU), celebrated the strike as a show of support for 'the massive revolutionary uprising' around Iran.[1] On 16 November, the workers continued their strike, this time organising a mass rally in the factory.[2] They shouted threatening slogans: 'We will come out every day, don't you think it's only one day', and 'If our problem is not solved, the factory will shut down.'[3] The mammoth factory had stopped working: the trucks lay filled with products that were not being moved and the assembly lines had no one to operate them. The workers were flaunting their power. They went back to work on 17 November but sporadic strike action was to follow in the days to come. From 26 to 29 November, many Isfahan steelworkers walked off the job, this time with the support of others who were inspired by them: from truck drivers who refused to carry the products from the factory to autoworkers who joined them in solidarity. They also inspired strike action in other parts of the country. On 29 November it was the turn of workers at the pellet factory in Madkush, near Bandar Abbas, the main Iranian port on the Persian Gulf.[4] On 1 December, when President Raisi visited the restive Kurdistan, he faced a province where many shops were closed in protest and hundreds of transport workers had gone on strike.

Before the strike, their employers had rung them up – warning them of severe consequences. But they refused to be intimidated.[5]

The authorities weren't bluffing. Some workers across the country, like steelworkers in the Rasht Industrial Complex, were met with suspension or expulsion because of their role in the strikes. Yet the strike wave continued to swell. Strikes even spread to one industry that always disconcerted the regime: oil. On 4 December, around five hundred contract workers at oil terminal and storage facilities went on strike in Mahshahr, Khuzestan.[6] They asked for better wages and benefits and similar terms to permanent workers. They made national and international headlines, with commentators inevitably summoning the spectre of 1979 oil strikes. This revealed their own optimism rather than reality: unlike 1979, the contract workers now striking were only a tiny sliver of the massive ranks of the Iranian oil workers. But it reminded the world of workers' untapped power.

A day later, this power grabbed the spotlight as a three-day strike began across the country. In Tehran, Seyf Khodro autoworkers were among the first to walk out. Working without pay for ten months, their anger reverberated throughout the nation. Also downing tools were the workers of Tehran-based Darugar, the shampoo company known to most Iranians by its hygiene products and its palm tree logo. Further to the south, Arak, an industrial stronghold, saw strike action by petrochemical workers. On the outskirts of Isfahan, the steelworkers were now joined by cement workers who came out in equally impressive numbers. With its seventeenth-century blue-tiled mosques and exemplary copper handicrafts, Isfahan has long been known as a tourist hotspot for Iranians and foreigners alike. But it was now the epicentre of a strike belt and looked more like Vyborg than Florence.[7]

On the coast of the Persian Gulf, Mahshahr oil workers were joined by other contract workers in the industry participating in the three-day strike. Further east, near Bandar Abbas, workers of the massive Almahdi Aluminium factory came out in droves. Truck workers, so essential to supply chains, also joined the strike in many places.

No one was surprised that the strike had some of its strongest turnouts in Kurdistan. Kurds are more politically organised and more to the left than most other Iranians; the decade after the 1979 revolution was marked by armed struggle by far left groups in Iranian Kurdistan. In Sanandaj, petrochemical workers came out. All over the province, shopkeepers joined the strikes too. Videos displaying entire rows of closed shops and bazaars testified to a province in a near-total shutdown.

Similar strike actions were taken by workers and shopkeepers all over Iran. By one count, at least forty-five cities joined the strike in one way or another. From the subtropical Chabahar port near the Pakistani border to balmy Lahijan on the Caspian Sea, and everywhere in between, Iranians had attempted to show their determination to carry the movement forward.

In the big cities like Tehran, even some upmarket pizzerias and shoe stores showed solidarity in their own way: they remained nominally open but silently asked customers to not buy anything. They were trying to do their part without incurring the full wrath of the authorities.

Retribution was real and swift. Shops that were closed between 5 and 7 December were marked by threatening slogans, scribbled in red paint by pro-regime vandals. One, painted on the windows of a striking car tyre shop in Tehran, read: 'Down with the shopkeeper who sold his country. You are being monitored.'[8] The phrase 'you are being monitored' was posted on many shops. In the days to come, some of the shops involved in the strike lost their licence to operate.

The last day of the strike, 7 December, coincided with the Students Day, commemorating the three left-wing students who were killed by the army in 1953 when they came out to protest an impending visit to Tehran by then Vice President Richard Nixon. Using the occasion, the workers declared their solidarity with students.

'This year's Students Day is a massive and historical day for solidarity between workers, teachers, women, students and oppressed masses of Iran, as crystallised in three days of strikes and street protests,' IIWU thundered in a statement. 'It will be a step forward for the nation-wide uprising of Iranian people for freedom and equality.'[9] Tehran's Bus Workers Union joined in by declaring support for 'students and other oppressed groups.'[10]

Yet, impressive as the three-day action was, it was far from a general strike that could truly shut society down. The workers had flexed their muscles but it would take much more to bring serious blows on the regime. Years of Western-imposed sanctions had weakened domestic industries and destroyed standards of living of the working class. In the limited imagination of some comfortably-off commentators, this meant that workers were 'fed up' and ready to revolt. But workers themselves understood the high stakes involved – striking without job security and meagre savings was a risk they were reluctant to accept.

Furthermore trade union and other forms of workers' organisations had been consistently suppressed for decades. They existed in only a few industries. As the regime's various factions – reformists, centrists and conservatives – had fought ferociously for years, none of them had given much support to trade unions or prioritised their campaigns. Trade unions struck all of them as a nuisance at best. Many of those who advocated socially or politically liberal policies fiercely opposed trade union struggles against privatisations, 'rationalisations' and other 'structural adjustments', i.e. the neoliberal playbook. No faction had an economic philosophy with room for workers' demands.

Consequently there was little appreciation of working-class power, methods and aims amongst many well-off supporters of the revolution. Iran's middle-class revolutionaries frequently associated the 'working class' with the rural or urban poor – a base for conservatives like Ahmadinejad, not the harbingers of the regime's overthrow. While these 'revolutionaries' could sloganeer about *etesaab* (a strike), they neither understood its power nor its mechanics. Street fights with the police and crowds struck them as more radical than workers downing tools. The lack of a powerful nationwide trade union movement, combined with affluent progressives' incomprehension, relegated trade unions to the margins of popular political consciousness and prevented further growth. Yet trade unions persisted – and their actions bore witness to their latent potential. Even if they were limited to a handful of industries, they had become a fixture of political life in the country. Veteran activists could well remember days when things were worse.

* * *

Almost exactly twenty years before the strikes of 2022, the Iranian trade union movement rose from the dead. A perfect venue was chosen: a funeral.

On 16 October 2002, Hossein Semnani passed away at the age of seventy-two. Semnani was the leader of the Shoemakers' Union and a long-time veteran of the workers' movement. In the 1950s, he had been a member of the communist Tudeh Party of Iran and a leading figure of its associated Central Council of United Trade Unions (CCUTU) which, at its height, organised 400,000 workers. Semnani had been like a living memory for the workers' movement. In 1953, when a US-backed coup brought down Prime Minister Mohammad Mossadegh, and the authorities and their violent supporters waged a ferocious campaign of repression against Tudeh and CCUTU, Semnani was among those who were arrested. Released after a few months, he sustained the Shoemakers' Union in those bleak times, writing practical trade union pamphlets that continue to be popular. Alongside most other organisations outside the regime's control, Iranian trade unions had been mostly shut down by the early 1980s. But Semnani's life and work continued to inspire.[11]

Semnani's funeral brought together many stalwarts of the workers' movement. On his gravestone, a couplet by communist martyr Mohammad Farokhi Yazdi spoke to the mood: 'On the day of my death, do not seek my face in the dust; for in the hearts of the wise rests my shrine.'[12] This was the Persian-language equivalent of the famed slogan of Swedish-American trade unionist Joe Hill: 'Don't mourn, organise.' As activists gathered to commemorate Semnani, they put this axiom into practice. Now they asked: could the trade unions be revived?

Ever since Khatami was elected in 1997 on a pro-reform platform, civil society organisations had mushroomed across Iran. They mobilised activists to push for democratic reforms and other political rights. President Khatami championed 'civil society', deploying these groups as a tool to push back against the conservative establishment. But independent trade unions lagged behind and lacked advocates among the reformists within the regime. These reformists controlled the state-controlled unions (called the House of Labour) and had no intention of tolerating a challenge from rank-and-file workers in the industrial sphere.

Semnani's funeral led to a chain of meetings where veterans of the workers' movement met younger workers. At first, they were mostly reminiscing about the heroism of Semnani and his comrades in the old days. Soon, discussions became more action-orientated. Now that Iran was going through a democratic upheaval, could the labour movement raise its head again? Practical plans were discussed for sectors that had once had strong labour organisations. Before long several trade unions sprung back into action. A new chapter had opened.

* * *

Tehran is notorious for its bumper-to-bumper traffic jams, clogging the city's arteries and making getting around impossible. But on 25 December 2005, Tehranis were witness to more than the usual traffic chaos. All the major streets of the city were impassable. The city's main north-south road, Valiasr Avenue, was shut to traffic along much of its eighteen kilometres. A headline at the pro-regime Mehr News Agency said it all: 'Strike by bus drivers paralyses Tehran.'[13]

For proponents of democracy, 2005 had been a horrifying year. After Mahmoud Ahmadinejad was inaugurated in August, his hard-line administration lost no time in cracking down. One victim of these measures was the Tehran Bus Workers Union, officially refounded in 2004 after its suppression in 1981. Organising fifteen thousand bus drivers, drivers' assistants, ticket sellers and technical workers, the union now unleashed its power. It took the Ahmadinejad administration by surprise – scrambling in the wake of the downtrodden workers it claimed to represent.

And the bus workers didn't stand alone. About a dozen trade unions stepped back onto the public stage in the mid-2000s. The days of dormancy were over. How did a strike on such a grand scale happen? The Bus Workers Union benefitted from the charisma of its leader, Mansoor Osanloo, who had worked as a bus driver since 1984. He came from a trade unionist family: his father, uncle and other relatives had helped organise workers in places such as Varamin's sugar-cube factory and the national oil company.[14] Throughout his long years at the bus company, he had been something of a trade unionist without a trade union. Although the union had been effectively non-existent since 1981, Osanloo always spoke to his fellow drivers about the rights their predecessors had won in the 1960s. These included benefits such as the daily provision of milk and cake and semi-annual provision of a suit and trousers (Iran's choice formal dress, necessary for weddings and funerals, which could be prohibitively expensive for the average worker).

In 2004, as the efforts for trade union revival ballooned around the country, there was no doubt that Osanloo would be the prime candidate to lead his fellow bus workers. The union started by holding meetings in a *Hosseyniyeh*, a congregation hall primarily for commemorating the martyrdom of Hussein, the third Shia Imam. The Hosseyniyeh in Tehran's Hassanabad Square belonged to the Bakers Guild.[15] Guilds had deep roots in Iranian history, going back to the medieval Seljuk dynasty. They were traditionally bazaar organisations that had brought together all shopkeepers of a certain trade, say goldsmiths or herbalists. With time, some workers had also organised their own guilds. Hence the

Bakers Guild was the closest thing to a trade union still standing in the eighties and nineties.

In addition to meetings, the union also used the Hosseyniyeh for holding classes. Activists, usually bus drivers themselves, taught their fellow workers about the history of trade unions, the impact of austerity policies around the world and the rights workers could demand under Iran's labour code and constitution. The classes weren't simply educational, they were a foundation for future organising. Bus workers now had a space to compare notes about conditions and routes and to make connections across the city.

The blowback was predictable and severe. On 9 May, thugs attacked the union's office and beat up anybody there with batons and clubs. They also stole the union's documents. But this brutal assault only steeled the union's resolve. Just a few weeks later, thousands of bus workers came together to proclaim the revival of the union. They represented drivers from every single district of Tehran.

Osanloo quickly emerged as a national figure. His rise was refreshing to those disillusioned with the failure of the Khatami years. If liberal activists loved to cite chapter and verse of jargon-filled human rights codes, Osanloo spoke in a way that resonated with ordinary Iranians.

In September 2008, after one of his many arrests, he gave a memorable speech to a gathering of drivers.

'When they took me to the intelligence ministry,' Osanloo said. 'I told them what I will also tell you now. I told the interrogator: "You want to interrogate me? Hear my words! I made the revolution in 1979. I made the revolution to have independence, to have freedom, to have social justice. But now our daughters are taken for prostitution to Dubai, Islamabad, Karachi and Kuwait, compelled by poverty... the interrogator put his head down in shame.'"[16]

If middle-class activists liked to quote Gandhi, Osanloo invoked the long traditions of Islamic socialism by quoting Ali, the first Shia Imam. 'It is Ali who said that when poverty enters the house, faith leaves! We don't need to be poor. Our country is rich, let's unite and fight for our rights.'

Osanloo's speech made the rounds on the internet, frequently edited with songs and symbols from the labour movement. Students and journalists now rushed to put their services at the behest of a new growing union movement.

There was even a fresh trade union anthem, written to the tune of *Cancion del mariachi* by Antonio Banderas and Los Lobos, a sound track from the 1995 neo-western action film *Desperado*. Its lyrics spoke to the new confidence of the union movement:[17]

You government people, you upper class ones,
We want a union!
We are done with working ourselves to death,
We want a union!
We want a union for our lives, for our kids
We want a union for our wages, for our dignity!
Oh yeah, we want a union! We won't sit silent.
We don't have villas in Dubai or Canada,
We work like dogs but we have no future,
How do you think you could ever scare us?

Arrested in December 2005, Osanloo spent eight months in jail. In the years to come, he was repeatedly arrested, beaten up and tortured. It was clear that his life could be in danger. Apart from being regularly roughed up by the authorities, he often got death threats on the phone. Once, he was even attacked in public by an unknown group. In 2013 he finally left for Turkey and then the US. But his shoes were filled almost immediately. The union threw up one inspiring leader after another: Ebrahim Maddadi, Davud Razavi, Reza Shahabi and Farahnaz Shiri. Farahnaz was Tehran's first woman bus driver, fired multiple times in retaliation for her union organising. She attempted to get her job back through filing lawsuits – unwilling to give up a profession she had started as a teenager. She, like bus workers across Tehran, was ready for a fight.[18]

* * *

All over Iran, trade union struggles sprung to life. Arak, a few hours south of Tehran, was a traditional working class city. Its population mainly consisted of the offspring of domestic migrants who had rushed to the city in the 1960s and 70s to help build up its industrial behemoths.* Chief among them was the Heavy Equipment Production Company, known by its acronym HEPCO. Founded in 1972, it was the first manufacturer of heavy

---

* This included families of my paternal grandfather and grandmother who moved there from central Iran. My father was born in Arak and most of my paternal relatives still live there.

76

machinery in the Middle East and the largest, responsible for building earthmovers, harvesters, cranes and trucks, essential for a modernising country. But by 2005 it was in decline. In 2006, its management passed to a regime insider who a year later benefitted from the privatisation policies that had gone on under both Khatami and Ahmadinejad and bought the company on the cheap. He started selling the core machinery and firing workers. The workers waged a campaign demanding workers' control and a limit on importing the heavy machinery from abroad.[19] This struggle was only the tip of the iceberg.

Teachers were part of this reinvigorated workers' movement. They first used the existing guild associations and also founded the Teachers' Organisation of Iran, politically close to pro-Khatami reformists. But when even their most basic demands, such as inflation-adjusted wage raises, were stymied, they grew bolder. Teachers in five major provinces came together to form a new Coordinating Council and organised a demonstration of more than 6,000 teachers outside parliament in early 2007. As police forces surrounded them, one of their chants announced their own power: 'Hey cops! You too were once our pupils.'

The working class rose up everywhere, cutting across all divides. To this day, teachers continue to protest Islamist ideologies being forced on themselves and the students, the expansion of private schools and the commodification of education.

Workers' struggles were also increasingly coordinated across different occupations. Starting life as a union for the unemployed,

IIWU took its current name in 2009 to represent the new union movement as a whole. In the run-up to Nowruz in March 2013, it helped gather forty thousand signatures for a petition to the labour minister, asking for the minimum wage to be increased in line with inflation.[20] Workers in all sorts of industries supported the campaign: carpet workshops in Isfahan, tile factories in Yazd and car tyre factories in Karaj, nurses and paramedics in Tehran, railway workers in Yazd and petrochemical workers in the Persian Gulf. They weren't only asking for a real raise in the minimum wage, which had not kept up with inflation since it was introduced, but protesting against the plague of temporary and irregular contracts and the non-payment of wages. These protests, demanding a higher minimum wage, are now an annual fixture in the Iranian political calendar.

The new union movement also produced a vibrant cultural renaissance. Events hosted by the metalworkers' union screened left-wing films appealing to ordinary workers. Favourites included Stanley Kubrick's 1960 epic *Spartacus* with its themes of slave revolt and charismatic leadership; Charlie Chaplin's semi-silent 1936 satire *Modern Times* with its critique of capitalism; and Michael Moore's 2007 documentary *Sicko*, which hit home with its railing against for-profit health care – long the norm in the US but also increasingly promoted in Iran.[21]

In early 2010, as Iran was engulfed in a mass uprising following the rigged presidential elections the year before, four trade unions came together to publish a charter for the Minimum Demands of Workers of Iran.[22] Workers were now speaking for themselves, fighting for their own demands and pursuing their own goals.

* * *

But to find the real epicentre of Iran's new trade union movement, we have to look beyond the industrial giants in teeming cities. We need to go to a corner of the southwestern Khuzestan province near the border with Iraq. This site is the margin of the margins, not only far from Tehran and Isfahan, but ninety minutes away from Khuzestan's provincial centre, Ahvaz. For most Iranians, the only reason they might make the trip is to visit the magnificent Chogha Zanbil, an ancient complex nearby, built in 1250 BC by the Elamite King Untash-Napirisha. Also nearby lies the city of Shush, now a small town but once a centre of Elamite civilisation and the winter capital of the fabled Persian Empire of the Achaemenid Dynasty; a city mentioned in the Bible and home to the final resting place of Daniel, the Hebrew prophet.*

Right between Shush and Chogha Zanbil, lie sugarcane fields cultivated by the mighty river of Karkhe and forming an area called Seven Hills or Haft-Tappeh. Intent on establishing Iran's first sugar factory, the Shah had developed the Haft-Tappeh Agribusiness Complex in the 1970s, after forcing the local people

---

* Six cities in the region claim to host the titular protagonist of the Book of Daniel. My wife's hometown of Mersin, Turkey, stands among them and she insists that it's the only 'real' one.

to sell their land and work for the new company. The new business soon flourished. Most Iranians drink several cups of tea a day, often with copious amounts of sugar. Now Iran could finally produce the sugar itself, reducing reliance on imports. It also provided a solid livelihood for the people of Shush and its surroundings. This neglected area, millennia away from its past glory in antiquity, now pulsed with life again. Housing 7,000 workers, Haft-Tappeh rapidly evolved into a small town. It had its own cinema, stadium, hospital and schools. By the late 1970s, unemployment was a thing of the past for this corner of Khuzestan. The factory produced an astonishing 100,000 tonnes of sugar a year.

Even the 1979 revolution and the eight-year war with Iraq in the 1980s didn't shut Haft-Tappeh down. It famously didn't cease production for a single day throughout the long years of the war, even when it was hit by Iraqi bombers. After the war, many ex-soldiers went back to cutting canes and producing sugar products for Haft-Tappeh.

Until the late 1990s, Haft-Tappeh continued to thrive. Ever since its foundation, the finance ministry had simply bought all of its sugar at a fixed price that allowed its workers to make a decent living. The agribusiness employed workers on all levels: there were seasonal workers who came to cut the canes, those who crushed the stalks and those who helped transport it. It still produced 100,000 tonnes of sugar as well as tens of thousands of tonnes of associated products such as molasses and bagasse. Even the natural fibre that was left after the production was sold as animal feed and helped make paper and wood products. There were facilities on site to process sugar to make alcohol or baker's yeast.

But in the late 1990s, as the Khatami administration started liberalising society, its economic cronies went after state-owned industries such as Haft-Tappeh. In 1999, the finance ministry shocked the workers by annulling its purchase contract. Iran now relied on cheap imported sugar. Later, it turned out that this move had benefitted politically connected businessmen who imported sugar from top global producers in Brazil and India and even the United Arab Emirates, which had once relied on Iran for much of its food. The Sugar Mafia soon turned out to be linked to the office of a leading Grand Ayatollah in Qom.

This was a devastating blow to Haft-Tappeh. The company's staff knew everything about producing sugar and other products but had never had to sell it in the global market, so distant from this corner of Khuzestan. Two thousand workers soon lost their jobs. Khatami's privatisation initiatives led to similar layoffs hitting other industries such as the textile factories of Isfahan. But in the big cities like Tehran or Isfahan, workers could move to other jobs. For Haft-Tappeh workers, losing their jobs meant unemployment and immediate economic ruin. Now, even those who remained employed often didn't get paid for months on end.

But with the union movement growing, Haft-Tappeh workers got new ideas. Starting in 2005, they began demonstrating with a simple slogan: 'We are the workers of Haft-Tappeh. We are hungry.'[23] Millions of Iranians had tasted the sweet sugar made by the toilers of Haft-Tappeh but few knew anything about their hunger. This was to now change. In 2007, things moved to a new phase. The 4,000 workers remaining organised regular mass meetings in the factory, marched in front of the provincial governor's office in Ahvaz and even closed off provincial roads. In November, 2,500 workers, a clear majority, wrote a letter to provincial labour ministry officials and asked for a revival of their trade union that had originally been founded in 1974. Organisers of the campaign were swiftly arrested but the union was now a reality. On May Day 2008, it announced its official re-establishment. The workers started a new campaign and asked for back pay for their unpaid wages, cessation of prosecution against union activists, a change in the company management, expulsion of the head of the security and recognition of the trade union. The workers also stood resolutely against all plans for privatisation of the company.

The Haft-Tappeh struggle inspired many around the country. The workers deployed a diversity of tactics including strikes, demonstrations in front of provincial government offices and organising supporters in cities near and far. The tough conditions of workers soon became well-known in the press. Many now knew about the life of seasonal cane cutters who worked for six hot months, often cutting their hands and getting sick from the vapour the canes released. Workers were able to delay privatisation and win some of their short-term demands.

The union also gave rise to recognised workers' leaders. With his big grey moustache, broad shoulders and red T-shirts, Ali Nejati, the union's president, looked like an Iranian Lech Wałęsa. Tried in early 2009 alongside four other members of the union's board, he was convicted of 'propaganda against the regime' and sentenced to six months in prison.[24] He has since spent years in and out of jail for crimes such as being in touch with activists aboard, organising demonstrations on May Day and International Women's Day, opening a workers' library in the city of Andimeshk and organising weekly union meetings.

But the regime officials soon found out that jailing Nejati and other union leaders couldn't shut the union down. New generations of workers' leaders and their supporters emerged. Born in 1983, Esmayil Bakhshi had lived his entire life under the Islamic Republic. He was a local boy, hailing from Dezful, Khuzestan's second biggest city. His Dezfuli accent, with its slow and sympathetic ring, was unmissable. He had worked his entire adult life for Haft-Tappeh. Organisers like Esmayil have long been the nightmares of governments and bosses because it is very hard to brand them as outside agitators. He talked and walked like the local boy that he was.

From its election in 2013, the administration of Hassan Rouhani had never promised to be worker-friendly. In fact, it was staunchly pro-business and its economic advisers loved to sing the praise of austerity politics. In his pre-presidency publications, Rouhani had railed against trade unions as harmful to free markets.[25] Nevertheless, Iranians had voted in droves for

Rouhani, chiefly for his promise of reaching a diplomatic reconciliation with the United States that could help ease the sanctions on Iran. When that deal was reached in 2015, following months of intense negotiations in Muscat, Geneva, Lausanne and Vienna, the Iranian economy had a shot at doing better. But hopes were dashed a year later, when Donald Trump was elected president and prepared to smash the Iran deal, alongside most diplomatic achievements of his predecessor, Barack Obama. Although Rouhani was re-elected in 2017, it soon became clear that he wouldn't be able to realise his lofty promises.

In December 2017, a new wave of revolt spread all over the country. This was the biggest protest wave since 2009. Unlike the previous movements which were led by the middle class, this time the protagonists were the lower classes who came out with economic demands. Haft-Tappeh workers, who were already in the midst of a strike when the revolt began, set the tune in northern Khuzestan. Throughout 2018, the province bore witness to an ongoing proletarian revolt, chiefly led by the workers of Haft-Tappeh and the National Steel Company in Ahvaz.

Bakhshi now rose as a labour leader of national renown. In a country whose politics was often dominated by the 1979 generation, the thirty-five-year-old Dezfuli unionist cut an attractive figure. In one of this better-known speeches from November 2018, Bakhshi broke into tears as he said: 'Four workers set themselves of fire. For the want of 12 million rials. Damn this life'.[26] 'Damn this life' soon became a slogan for Iranians fed up with their rapidly declining standards of living.

In another speech from the same month, Bakhshi is heard speaking to the workers just after they've welcomed him with a traditional Shia chant: 'Oh Allah, may you grant peace and honour on Muhammad and his household.' 'This is what a workers' meeting means,' he said. 'Here, right here, we the workers ourselves decide our own fate and our own demands. We issue our commands from below. We've had enough of being struck on the head from the above.'[27]

Bakhshi was soon not only beloved by his fellow Haft-Tappeh workers but hailed in demonstrations across the province. The regime's usual tactics to crush opponents wouldn't work. In early 2017, he had been hauled off a bus by hired gangsters and beaten to a pulp, breaking his collarbone. Yet he kept up the struggle.

In early 2019, following another strike, he openly detailed the torture he had gone through in prison, leading to a national and international outcry. The regime now went back to its tested playbook: it broadcast a nineteen-minute 'documentary' on state media that painted a hackneyed picture of a conspiracy plot involving Trump, Netanyahu and a Marxist centre in Sweden who had allegedly worked together to bring about labour strikes in Iran.[28] Using the regime's method of choice – forced confessions extracted by torture – the report aired statements by Bakhshi and Sepideh Qolian, a young journalist and a fellow Dezfuli who had become a well-known activist for the cause of Haft-Tappeh. Millions watched as Bakhshi and Qolian admitted to everything and denied torture on national TV. But this time, the labour activists had outsmarted their torturers. Soon after the TV documentary aired, a video emerged of Qolian, recorded in between two rounds of her arrests, in which she described all the torture she had gone through.[29] She also revealed that she and Bakhshi had been forced to record confessions. Responding to allegations about her being left-wing, she defiantly said: 'Has the Iranian constitution banned being a communist?'

By the 2022 revolt, Iranian trade unionism burned brightly – a far cry from where it was at the start of this millennium. Today it can boast of seasoned activists, hard-fought industrial disputes and an energetic rank-and-file. Now Iranian workers are in pole position to force their own goals through.

* * *

As Iranians staged a new revolutionary movement in 2022 and 2023, they became more conscious of why labour organisations matter. Trade unions like those led by Tehran bus workers and Haft-Tappeh sugarcane workers are now household names.

Haft-Tappeh continues to be a major force. In February 2023, it joined eighteen other organisations in launching a Charter of Minimum Demands for Independent Civil and Guild Organisations of Iran. In March, Bakhshi was seen on the grave of Kian Pirfalak, a nine-year-old child from Khuzestan who was killed by government forces on 16 November, 2022, as they clashed with protesters in Izeh.[30] Kian had touched many hearts around the world when a video emerged of him talking about his dream of becoming a robotics engineer. In the clip, as he is sending a handmade boat to a school student festival, Kian starts his words with a phrase that now became an emblem of the revolution: In the Name of the God of Rainbows. If the regime's God was a murderous tyrant, a revolution was now fighting it in the name of the colours of the rainbow.

On 16 March, as the tide of the movement had slowed down, Bakhshi joined Kian's family by a visit to his grave. Kian's parents and uncle now stood next to their fellow Khuzestani, his mother wearing a cap that barely covered her hair. It was an obvious sign of revolutionary resilience.

Sitting on a small plastic bench, Bakhshi spoke sternly: 'We have painted our face red with Kian's blood, promising that we won't ever forget. Whenever we look into the mirror, we must know our duty. We must know what we are fighting for and we must not forget all the blood that was shed.'

Bakhshi came with a message from a group of Haft-Tappeh workers, addressed to Kian: 'Dear Kian, we are here to speak of our shame. It was us who should have been killed on the streets so that you could reach all your dreams. But it wasn't to be. We promise to continue the struggle to build a world and a future for your friends, filled with joy and freedom.'

Four

The Cheetah Who Died for the Revolution: The Fight for the Environment

On the morning of 28 February 2023, Iranians woke up to the news of the heartbreaking death of Pirouz, another casualty of the regime. Months into a national uprising that had seen hundreds of protesters killed on streets, Iranians had grown accustomed to mourning. But this was different.

Pirouz was a Persian cheetah, a critically endangered subspecies. At ten months old, he died of kidney failure just before 7 a.m.

The entire nation grieved; laments poured in from all corners. A footballer declared it a 'great national catastrophe' and a time for 'national mourning'. A TV anchor published a photograph of him staring wistfully at the camera and wrote: 'We lost Pirouz too. Look at his eyes, full of wondering, dreams and remorse. Doesn't he look like all of us?' There was hardly an Iranian in the public eye who didn't say something about it. Media outlets were soon flooded with op-eds and think pieces about what it all meant. From his exile in the US, former crown prince Reza Pahlavi called Pirouz's painful death a sign of the 'regime's incompetence and cruelty'.

'For myself and millions of Iranians, Pirouz was a sign of hope,' Pahlavi tweeted. 'Those who thought that they can kill death and hopes in our hearts should know that we will be ever more determined. We will take back Iran and build it anew.'[1]

Pirouz's life had been avidly followed by millions of Iranians since the day he was born. His mother, Iran, had been rescued in 2017 from the hands of a Tehrani animal-trafficking gang. Years of treatment and attempts to impregnate her continued in Tehran's Centre for Reproduction of Persian Cheetahs. But they didn't work and in 2020 she was finally returned to her birthplace, the Tooran National Park in Semnan province.[2] There the reproduction effort pressed on. The hope was that Iran could mate with Kooshki, a fellow Persian cheetah donated by a hunter years ago. But Kooshki was now fifteen years old and he was not up to the job. This is where Firouz, a ten-year-old cheetah, came in. Having been found in the wild, he was sent to Tooran in 2021. Iran was at first afraid of this male cheetah, a few years her senior. But trainers taught Firouz how to be more gentle. At long last they successfully mated and Iran became pregnant. On 1 May 2022, she gave birth to three cubs, who became instant celebrities. Two passed away quickly but Pirouz survived. Experts from both Iran and South Africa tended to him in a specialist centre in Tehran. He was given quality chicken, veal and supplements and weighed 4.5 kilograms five months in. This cub embodied the hopes of the nation. But that fateful February morning dashed them all.

This sorrowful keening for a big cat might seem bizarre or even histrionic. Jaded observers bemoaned the fact that dead humans hadn't received half the attention of young Pirouz. Why care about a big cat in the middle of a revolution?

But anybody paying attention knew why Pirouz counted as a martyr for the revolution. When Iranians rallied under the slogan 'Women, Life, Freedom', they were fighting for the protection of Iran's environment and the right of its native species to flourish.

The fate of Persian cheetahs epitomised decades of wanton environmental destruction. Primarily known as Asiatic cheetahs, these big cats came from the deserts of Turkmenistan and once roamed everywhere from the Arabian Peninsula to the Caucasus and northern India. But they were hunted close to extinction and hardly any remain, being found only in central Iran. Iranians have hence adopted them as Persian cheetahs and made them their national symbol – emblazoned on the football team's World Cup jerseys.

This embrace of a critically endangered species flows freely from Iranians' struggle against worsening environmental problems. As Iranians confront an unaccountable regime, its lack of care for the country's natural ecosystems typifies the deadly collision between corrupt business interests and an ineffective state – a collision that harms Iranians in all spheres of their lives.

The gradual extinction of the Persian cheetah made many Iranians feel like their country was collapsing before their eyes. As late as 2013, more than eighty individuals had been sighted in the country. But by the time of Pirouz's death, the Iranian authorities believed that only twelve survived. Many other species have suffered this slow demise. The Persian onager has a deep place in Iranian mythology, literature and history. Bahram V, a Sassanian king of the fifth century, was known as Bahram the Onager for his love of hunting this animal. But today it is endangered. Only a few hundred remain of the subspecies, many of whom are in zoos or reserves in Germany, the United States, Israel or Saudi Arabia.

The disappearance of onagers and cheetahs is only one item on a long list of environmental disasters. Isfahan, the fabled capital city of the Safavids, is known for the magnificent bridges over the Zayandeh river, the largest waterway of the Iranian plateau. But since around 2007 the river is often dry in much of its course. Lake Urmia, in northwestern Iran, is the sixth biggest salt lake in the world. It is a natural wonder known for its flamingos, pelicans, spoonbills and the endangered Persian fallow deer. It encompasses more than a hundred islands with hundreds of residents, the most famous of whom is the stuff of myths: Hulagu Khan, grandson of Genghis Khan and a Mongol ruler in his own right. Hulagu conquered much of the Middle East and sacked its cultural capital, Baghdad, in 1258, single-handedly putting an end to the Islamic Golden Age. But he died in Iranian lands and was allegedly buried on Lake Urmia's Shahi Island, although his tomb has never been found. Now the lake, one of Iran's key tourist destinations, has been gradually drying due to badly planned dams, highways and wasteful water usage. Few images are as depressing to Iranians than that of Isfahan's bridges passing over dried-up Lake Urmia and its deer carcasses.

This is not simply a blow to national pride, but a material problem. The country's water crisis means that people in big cities, especially Tehran, are often faced with water shortage issues. Myriad other problems, compounded by climate change, threaten Iran's environment.

On 28 September, when little-known singer Shervin Hajipour released a power ballad that went on to become the anthem of the Women, Life, Freedom movement, nobody was surprised that many of its lines related to the environment. Crowd-sourced from the tweets of Iranians, the song was called 'For the Sake Of' and offered a long list of the reasons for the uprising:

For the sake of this polluted air,
For the sake of [Tehran's] Valiasr Avenue and its dying trees,
For the sake of Pirouz and the threat of his extinction

This was a green revolution.

* * *

The roots of Iran's environmental efforts reach back decades. The country had had its own Environmental Protection Organisation (EPO) since January 1972, about a year after President Nixon founded the USA's counterpart. Its founder, Eskandar Firouz, was a legendary figure. Hailing from a branch of the Qajar dynasty, he had once been an MP and a professional hunter who experienced a Damascene conversion on a trip to Africa in 1967. Eskandar arrived to hunt lions and elephants but suddenly found himself disgusted with the idea and started taking their pictures instead. He then helped turn Iran's Hunting Club (a favourite of the Shah) into the country's environmental organisation, the EPO. Firouz went on to establish Iran's first national parks and registries of protected wildlife refuges. He helped organise a historic convention in the resort city of Ramsar on the Caspian coast of Iran on 2 February 1971. Those present signed an international treaty for conservation and sustainable use of wetlands. UNESCO's list of wetlands of international importance are now called Ramsar Sites. To this day, the same name is used and 2 February is celebrated around the globe as the World Wetlands Day, although many have forgotten its Iranian origins.

Like almost anybody who held a government post under the Shah, Firouz was arrested after the 1979 revolution. Initially sentenced to execution, an intervention by a mysterious individual from Qom, whose name was never revealed, saved his life. His sentence was commuted to life in prison and in 1985, following almost seven years of imprisonment, he came out and could mentor a new generation of environmentalists.

There was no shortage of them. For most activists in Iran, the late 1990s were a new dawn, coinciding with reformist President Khatami's championing of civil society. But the environmentalists were ahead of the curve. By the time the new wave of civic activism hit the road, they had already been hard at work for years.

Ecological activism has a curious relationship to politics. Its targets can often be key economic and security interests, yet it portrays itself as benign and non-partisan. If a group, for instance, stands for clean rivers, what can be the justification in suppressing it? No one stands on a platform of championing dirty water.

In the late 1980s and early 1990s, as Iran was in the heat of a post-war reconstruction effort, environmental activists capitalised on this reputation as well-meaning but apolitical citizens to launch legal campaigns. In 1989, four medical students in Tehran founded the Green Front of Iran, which also went by the name Greenpeace, an obvious homage to the Vancouver-based global campaigning organisation.[3] In a society where civic activities had been severely limited for years, the Green Front offered a chance for ordinary people to take part in meaningful actions such as cleaning beaches and hiking routes, planting trees or protesting harmful development plans. It also organised family eco-tours and focused on getting young people and even children involved.[*] It made a habit of celebrating Earth Day in April and UN World Environment Day in June. The latter actually became an entire

---

[*] Admission: the author was a Green Front member in his early teens in Tehran.

Environment Week in Iran and dozens of events were held all over the country on its occasion. The Green Front soon boasted thousands of due-paying members. When the UN held the Earth Summit in Rio de Janeiro in June 1992, Iranian activists used resulting documents such as the Rio Declaration on Environment and Development to pursue their demands.

Green Front was hit badly in 2000 when a founding figure went to New York for a conference and decided to stay put in the United States. Like many Iranians, he had joined the 'brain drain' of the country's talented youth, looking for greener pastures in the West. But meanwhile, the movement had established new organisations and acquired a prized new addition: a charismatic figure.

With her snow-white hair, usually covered with a flimsy scarf, the septuagenarian Mahlaqa Mallah didn't immediately strike you as a trailblazing activist. But that's exactly who she was. Mahlaqa hailed from a long line of feminist activists stretching way back into the nineteenth century. Her grandmother, Bibi Khanoom Astarabadi, was a pioneering satirist who wrote passionately in defence of female education and founded the first modern school for girls in Iran. Clerics issued fatwas against her and opponents burnt her house down but Bibi Khanoom never wavered. Her daughter, Mahlaqa's mother, Khadije Afzal Vaziri, continued feminist activism and pursued her own journalistic career. Mahlaqa had grown up on such ideals and remembered her mother telling her never to back down in the face of bullies. After getting a doctorate in social sciences from the Sorbonne, she came back to work as a librarian in the

University of Tehran. That was when she first noticed the dearth of books on the environment and pollution.

Now in her seventies, she sensed a new opening and wanted to pursue what she had always regarded as the key to social change: women's participation and education. In 1994, she founded the Women's Society for Fighting Against Environmental Pollution (WSFAP).[4] The organisation had a catchy slogan: 'To teach one woman is to teach a nation.' It helped run classes on the environment for a wide range of women: some were house-wives and some were school teachers. Each could now pass on what they learned to many others, be it their own children or their pupils. Classes soon spread to sixteen provinces all over the country.

What made the organisation remarkable was its ability to bring together qualified experts, who could provide rigorous environmental knowledge, with activists who weren't afraid of rocking the boat. Mansoore Shojaee, a feminist advocate who joined WSFAP in 1996 at the age of thirty-eight, was a bit of both. An academic librarian like Mallah, she had lost her job when the regime's Cultural Revolution shut down all universities in 1980. But throughout the years she used her knowledge of French to translate and also wrote for the press. When the feminist move-ment revived in the 1990s, she became a devotee. Joining the leadership of WSFAP, Mansoore brought a distinct ecofeminist look that bridged the two nascent movements for women's rights and the environment. The books she wrote and translated on the ethics of ecology are still used by activists.

The activists brought their own methods. If the Green Front had petitioned obscure state bodies with polite environmental requests, the environmentalists now wanted to take bolder action in line with the zeitgeist. Prefiguring the youth-led climate rebellions of late 2010s, they organised kindergarten and primary school students who staged demonstrations against air pollution in Tehran, one of the most polluted cities in the world. The traditional Arbor Day in early March, where even regime leaders usually pose for a photo while planting a tree, now became a day of protest at the destruction of Iran's forests caused by unregulated construction projects.

But the increase in activism also brought its own challenges. As their work expanded, the environmentalists were now seen as a threat, not just by the regime but by many entrenched interests. Two particular causes led to serious warnings by the authorities. One was protests against nuclear plants which were soon to become the centre of a long-running diplomatic crisis for Iran. The other was protests against a motorway project planned to connect Tehran to Chalus, a popular resort town on the Caspian Sea. The project had been ongoing since 1974 – and it is still incomplete at the time of writing in 2023. Tehranis love to head north to the Caspian for long weekends and summer vacations but the 140-kilometre road between Tehran and Chalus can take three hours or more in busy periods. The motorway is supposed to cut this trip into half. But activists have long warned that the road could destroy protected areas and endanger species such as grey pelicans and the Caspian seals. WSFAP led some of the earliest protests against the motorway and even attempted to block the roads leading to Chalus.

Authorities soon called in Mallah, Shojaee and others and made it clear that these projects were red lines for the regime, and if activists continued, there would be consequences. The activists made a strategic retreat and chose to focus on other issues. But the movement they had helped jump-start has never stopped. In fact, buoyed by the vibrant journalistic scene that flourished in the early 2000s (even if many outlets were repeatedly closed down by the judiciary), environmentalism has become part and parcel of Iranian social and political life. Exposés and persistent local activism now routinely push the state authorities to take action. Construction magnates know they need to be worried about pesky environmentalists who will make them go viral for all the wrong reasons. In 2018, the semi-official Iranian Students News Agency (ISNA) published an exposé on the 'real estate bourgeoisie' linked to 'some of the authorities' who were 'profiting from destruction of the environment' by building villas in picturesque towns on Iran's Caspian coast.[5]

Even as state repression stamped out many media outlets, broadcasters based abroad have come to replace them. They dedicate hours of airtime to environmental issues and introducing people like Mahlaqa and Eskandar to new generations. Dire as the state of Iran's rivers, lakes and land continues to be, environmental issues now play a prominent part in Iran's political consciousness.

Environmental campaigns can now be found across the country's map. Bakhtegan, Iran's second largest internal lake after
Urmia, has its own active campaign[6] as do other threatened lakes
such as Hamoun and Maharloo. Criticisms of dams, once limited
to left-wing academics, have become much more widespread.
Many people now realise how dam-building can destroy birds
and fish, degrade river ecosystems and lead to the loss of forests,
wetlands and the erosion of deltas.

Nowhere was left untouched by environmental concerns. In
Khuzestan, local activists organised a campaign for millions of
Shia pilgrims who travel to Karbala in Iraq to make it there in
time for the occasion of the holy day of Arbaeen, which
commemorates forty days of mourning for the martyrdom of
Imam Hussein. As part of the Shia tradition, volunteers offer
copious amounts of food and drink to the pilgrims. An integral
part of the experience is having the delicious qeyme stew, made
with meat, yellow split peas and tomatoes and popular in both
Iran and Iraq, washed down with orange sherbet drinks. But
this also often means colossal environmental damage and
waste due to everything being provided with single-use cutlery,
cups and containers. But, launched in 2012, the Arbaeen
Without Footprints campaign encouraged pilgrims to reduce
their use of Styrofoam and single-use utensils by carrying their
own.[7] Hassan Nasser, a religious speaker and campaign
co-founder, gave nightly speeches during the Arbaeen with
titles such as 'Imam Hussein and the Environment'. Linking
the themes of ecological and social justice, he argued: 'If we

spend less money on single-use utensils, how many kids can we register in schools with that money? This is the true face of Islam and Arbaeen'.

The environmental movement had reached the devotees of Imam Hussein.

* * *

In 2013, the surprise victory of centrist Hassan Rouhani in the presidential elections put an end to eight tumultuous years of the conservative Ahmadinejad. Hopes for democratic change had been crushed but millions voted for Rouhani in hope of more social freedom and increased state competence. They also hoped for a stronger environmental policy. They wanted an end to the bleak years of a president who doled out favours to his cronies and ceded control of much of the state to unaccountable bodies, whose corruption inevitably included unscrupulous construction and foreign trade deals, often with disastrous consequences.

The most notable change came in the Environmental Protection Organisation. Masoume Ebtekar, who had held the job for eight years under Khatami (1997–2005) now returned to the helm under the new president. The American-educated Ebtekar had once been globally infamous for her role as the English-language spokeswoman of Islamist students who seized the US embassy in Tehran in 1979 and took American diplomats hostage. She had been dubbed Sister Mary, a nod to her scarf resembling a nun's habit. She never regretted her role in the hostage-taking affair or apologised for the ironic fact that her son went to get a PhD in the United States. But she had reinvented herself as the top environmental official of the Khatami government. Her father, who held a PhD in mechanical engineering from the University of Pennsylvania, had been appointed in 1979 as the second post-revolutionary head of the EPO. The daughter now got the job and expanded its remit.

Renewed hopes for the environment were on full display in early 2014 when a massive event brought together dozens of artists, economists, lawyers, athletes and civil society activists. The meeting adopted the title 'A Pact Between Civil Society and Authorities for a Blue Sky'.[8] In less flowery phrasing, it was intended as a reconciliation between environmentalists and the Rouhani government. The expression might strike you as corny but when Tehranis stared up at a sky darkened by soot and smoke, the resonance was obvious.

The meeting featured many celebrities. There was Maryam Toosi, the sprint athlete who held the Iranian record in several categories (100, 200, 400 and 4 x 400 metre relay) and had just won gold in the Asian Indoor Championships of Hangzhou. There were filmmakers and actresses, and high-profile professors and veterinarians.

Kambiz Norozi, a lawyer, attacked ministers of the Rouhani government for not attending the event and sending their deputies instead. Just a few years ago, Norozi had been sentenced to more than two years in prison and seventy-six blows of the lash. His outspoken words evinced the fearlessness of the post-2013 movement.

'The cabinet ministers, who don't give a damn for the people dying because of air pollution, won't be able to accomplish anything,' Noroozi said. 'We are living a disaster.'

The fieriest words came from University of Tehran's Professor Sadeq Zibakalam. Following up from Norozi, Zibakalam said: 'If this were a religious assembly broadcast on state TV, all the cabinet ministers would be here.'

'Our constitution has an article about the environment,' Zibakalam went on. 'But it means nothing! When the forests were burning in Gorgan [on the Caspian coast], we didn't even have helicopters to put the fires out. How much money is spent on military units while nothing is done to extinguish wildfires, to stop the drying up of rivers and lakes and to solve the air pollution problem?'[9]

Zibakalam then linked the terrible environmental record to the regime's disingenuous demagoguery.

'You know what we should do? We should tell everybody that Lake Urmia is in the United States,' he said. 'Because if it were there, Iran's state TV would dedicate a couple of primetime programmes to it every week. It would make dozens of documentaries about what a great catastrophe the lake drying out is. They would even talk about how it was an injustice done to Native and Black Americans while the American capitalists don't give a damn about it!'

Recognising the turpitude of a regime that claimed to fight the global imperialists while paying no heed to the country's own environment, the attendees gave Zibakalam a standing ovation.

But no one could rival the star power of the keynote speaker, introduced as 'the mother of the environmental movement of Iran': Mahlaqa Mallah. At the age of ninety-six, she still spoke with passion and clarity. She discussed the capital's pollution and condemned the sorry state of its factories and outdated cars. She repeated a demand she had made since the 1970s: that there should be a Ministry of the Environment. With her very presence, Mallah represented an unbroken thread of environmental activism.

The meeting ended with reading out a pact that had been signed by more than thirty thousand people. Ebtekar gave it her signature and promised that all cabinet ministers would sign it too. The Rouhani government promised to be pro-environment.

* * *

The government's environmentalism soon found a face that seemed to represent the best of what Iranians had hoped their government would deliver. Kaveh Madani bore no resemblance to a typically dour Iranian official. Born in Tehran in 1981, he had a BA from the University of Tabriz but had left Iran for postgraduate studies in Sweden and the United States. Madani's application of game theory to the thorny questions of water management had earned him widespread recognition. In 2017, he received the American Society of Civil Engineers' Walter L. Huber Prize, the most prestigious award for mid-career engineers.

Madani had never cut ties with Iran. Both of his parents had worked in the water sector and he had become a well-known authority on water, addressing the country's dire crisis, or to use his own term, 'water bankruptcy'. He lectured in Iran and gave a celebrated TEDx Talk recorded on Kish Island in 2015. He was the star of Al-Jazeera TV documentaries on the water crisis and dust storms of the Middle East.

In September 2017, Rouhani poached him from his teaching job at London's Imperial College. Madani would now become a vice president of Iran's Environmental Protection Organisation, where he would direct the education and research department.

Madani's recruitment sounded like a fairy tale. For many years, Iran had suffered from an acute case of brain drain. Iranian experts and students filled university departments around the world: from Western Europe and North America to India, Malaysia and the Philippines. Was there now hope that they could come back and serve their own country, welcomed by a president who pledged to restore 'Citizenship Rights' and value competence over devotion to the regime? Many hoped so while warily watching Madani's inauguration and struggles. Cynical old hands complained that Madani stood no chance against the established habits of the bureaucracy of the Islamic Republic. On the internet he was met with an onslaught of false accusations about his non-existent plans to divert water from provinces inhabited by non-Persian-speaking ethnicities. But Madani was seemingly unperturbed as he energetically organised his department and set out new plans. He waged a national campaign against waste and plastic pollution in Iran, engaging both ordinary social media users and celebrities. He also kept a constant presence on the circuit of international ecological forums and spoke of Iran's new ambitions in Nairobi, Paris and Bangkok. Maybe this young and bold scientist could be truly a face of change?

If it sounds too good to be true, that's because it was.[10] Early in 2018, the IRGC launched a new round of crackdown that targeted a set of internationally connected environmentalists. On 11 February, less than eight months into his new job, Madani was arrested. Able to leave prison shortly later, he quickly left Iran and resigned in absentia. He has never been back since.

But Madani's downfall had been only one aspect of the crackdown. A few days before, on 24 January, several environmental activists were arrested in a coordinated action that left even the Rouhani government dumbfounded. Rouhani's ministers swore to journalists that they had no idea about why the IRGC had gone ahead with these arrests.

Many of the arrested were connected to the Persian Wildlife Heritage Foundation (PWHF), a conservationist organisation focused on the Persian cheetah. The organisation had used its international ties and professional work ethics to achieve a lot in a short period: it published cutting-edge books on wildlife, it invested in scientific publications and conferences, it led awareness campaigns around conservation. It used the best practices of global organisations such as the United Nations Development Program and Panthera, a New York-based charity dedicated to preserving wild cats and their ecosystems.

Its head, Kavous Seyed Emami, was a soft-spoken sociologist with a PhD from the University of Oregon who held dual Iranian-Canadian citizenship. Seyed Emami was an instantly likable man. He wore his vast knowledge lightly, and anyone who met him on the eco-tours he organised could testify to his genuine fascination with nature. Like tens of thousands of Iranians, he had fought in the war with Saddam Hussein's Iraq in the 1980s, and had required hospitalisation after being injured by shrapnel. As he served as a faculty member in Tehran's Imam Sadiq University, a key regime institution, many expected him to be relatively safe from arbitrary repression.

But when the crackdown came, he was among the arrested. On 8 February, a few weeks later, he was found dead in his cell in Tehran's Evin prison. The regime claimed he had committed suicide. The country was in a state of total shock. No one believed that someone like Seyed Emami would kill himself. From New York, his son, the punk rock singer King Raam openly questioned the regime's narrative. Seyed Emami's students, friends, colleagues and family members all expressed similar sentiments. This was not a suicide.

The others arrested included similarly distinguished environmentalists, mostly involved with PWHF. You had Sepideh (Hamideh) Kashani and Hooman Jokar, a husband-and-wife duo known for their love for the environment and their trips to every corner of Iran. You had Taher Ghadirian who worked on a variety of big cat conservation projects. His passion had been for Pallas's cat, or manul, a small wild cat known for its dense grey fur and rounded ears. Amirhossein Khaleghi was focused on preventing poaching of the Persian cheetahs. Morad Tahbaz, perhaps the most charismatic among them, held Iranian, British and American citizenships, and had spent much of his wealth on wildlife preservation for years.

One of the youngest arrestees was Niloofar Bayani, only thirty-one years old at the time of her arrest. Niloofar had been born in Tehran but had left for Canada after high school. After studying at McGill for her undergraduate studies, she went to New York for an MA from Columbia University. She had also worked as a conservationist in Uganda and Tanzania before landing a job with the UN's Environment Programme in Geneva in 2012. In summer of 2017, buoyed by the promises of a new Iran, she had come home to work for PWHF.

Why had the IRGC rounded up environmentalists only interested in preserving big cats? The regime's own authorities soon came up with a familiar answer to this question. The environmentalists were accused of spying for the CIA and Mossad. The case was so scandalous that even the government's own Ministry of Intelligence openly declared that it didn't believe they were spies, exposing a divide between the security institutions.[11]

In kangaroo courts held in 2019 and 2020, they were sentenced to up to ten years in prison. Convictions were mostly based on confessions by Tahbaz and Bayani that had been clearly extracted under duress. The utter absurdity of the court was clear in some of its exchanges. Judge Abolqasem Salavati pointed to an email by Niloofar in which she had told Morad about experiencing 'burnout'. The judge claimed this term was a smoking gun and proved she was a spy who had been 'burnt'. One piece of supposed evidence used against her was proof that her mother had gone to Saudi Arabia, a state in a diplomatic conflict with Iran. Here the trial descended into farce: Niloofar's mother had gone there, like millions of devout Muslims, to perform the Hajj pilgrimage.

In September 2023, Tahbaz was released alongside four of his fellow Americans as part of a deal between Iran and the United States that involved releasing six billion dollars of blocked Iranian assets in South Korea. Niloofar and other environmentalists remain behind bars at the time of writing. The episode makes evidently clear that the regime practises an open policy of taking foreign citizens hostage and using them as bargaining chips in its dealings with the West. It furthermore proves the hollowness of the judicial process.

But years before the deal, even if there were any doubts about the forced nature of the confessions extracted from the environmentalists, they had been already put to rest when statements by Niloofar leaked to the media in February 2020. She spoke of at least 1,200 hours of interrogation by the IRGC with the aim of getting a forced confession from her.[12] According to her testimony, she had experienced 'the most severe form of psychological torture, and the threat of physical torture and sexual violence'. In letters to Khamenei and prison authorities, Niloofar detailed the mistreatment meted out to her by their men.

She had been taken to a private villa in leafy Lavasan, near Tehran, with seven armed men who proceeded to interrogate her for nine to twelve hours a day. They'd kick her in turns until she suffered from severe back pain. Ridiculing her conservation efforts, the IRGC interrogators asked Niloofar to imitate the sound of wild animals. Pulling up her sleeves, they held out an injection that could allegedly paralyse or kill her. They showed her the dead body of Seyed Emami, threatening to kill her and her family members. They asked her to fulfil their sexual fantasies. In Niloofar's account, much of this behaviour was filmed and could one day surface.

Three years later, in January 2023, statements by Sepideh Kashani further corroborated the allegations of torture. Interrogators had showed her footage of Seyed Emami's dead body too, she said. Accusing her of being a 'secret Bahá'í Jew', they'd repeatedly read her a fake execution decree for her husband, Hooman.

Yet Niloofar and Sepideh demonstrated that the regime could not break them – speaking out against the torture they experienced proved it. Standing steadfast in their beliefs, they enjoy the robust support of the Iranian civil society. In July 2022, a petition signed by three thousand academics, activists and lawyers, the leading lights of the environmental movement in Iran, demanded their release. Seven months later, the whole nation mourned for Pirouz. Their cause now touched the heart of Iranians everywhere.

In May 2023, another letter asked for the release of Niloofar and Sepideh. This one was signed by only twenty women – but each signature meant the world to the two prisoners. These signatories – including Faeze Hashemi, Narges Mohammadi, Sepideh Qolian and Bahare Hedayat – had shared prison cells with Sepideh and Niloofar. They knew them as sisters and comrades. They spoke of their cellmates as 'innocent lovers and servants of the environment' and praised their 'devoted and caring work for even the most remote ecosystems of Iran'.[13]

As they remain behind bars, Niloofar, Sepideh, Morad and all of Iran's incarcerated environmentalists have been vindicated.

Five

We Accuse! The Fight for Freedom of Expression

There's not much to see in Aybek, a rural district an hour's drive away from Tehran. The vast fields of wheat, barley, corn and alfalfa, all grown for Iran's mammoth capital, are hardly compelling tourist destinations. But on 20 November 2022, everyone's eyes were on Aybek. The Islamic Republic's security forces stormed the district, on a manhunt for Katayoun Riahi, a sixty-year-old actress who had been on the run for months. Her crime was her open support for the Women, Life, Freedom movement. The revolution now celebrated her as one of its own.

Katayoun had travelled an unlikely route to being a revolutionary icon. Born in a family of musicians and actors, she had
been only eighteen at the time of the 1979 revolution and hadn't
started acting yet, escaping from the repression that drove most
actresses into early retirement and even exile. The 1980s offered
few opportunities for a nascent star – the Iran-Iraq War dominated the post-revolutionary entertainment industry. It took
until the early 1990s for TV to open up, and Katayoun seized the
chance to make a name for herself. She landed a role in *The
Patriarch* (1993–95), the story of an elderly man who rules over
his family through a mixture of love, charisma and tyranny.
In the role of Zahra, the patriarch's eldest daughter-in-law,
Katayoun offered a permissible version of televised femininity:
smiling, kind and good-hearted to a fault. By 2001, her roles
were more transgressive. In *Last Supper* (2001), she starred as a
university professor who elopes with her daughter's love interest, played by a handsome actor fifteen years her junior. It was a
performance of a lifetime and showed just how quickly things
had changed in Iran's cinema scene.

Still Katayoun wasn't particularly daring. Like all other actors,
she knew that there were lines not to cross. One wrong move and
the Ministry of Culture and Islamic Guidance could finish your
career by banning you performing. Yet, Katayoun continued to
enjoy success, even on state television, whose head was directly
appointed by the Supreme Leader Khamenei. In 2008–9, she
even played the female lead in a major state-backed project by
pro-regime director Farajollah Salahsoor: *Prophet Joseph*, an

exceptionally expensive TV series based on the life of the biblical and Quranic prophet. She took the role of Zuleikha, the wife of a captain of Egyptian Pharaoh's guard, who falls for the young prophet's handsome looks at first sight. Katayoun was not a radical – she was the Iranian mainstream.

But, on 16 September 2022, only two days after Mahsa's death, Katayoun shocked the art world with an Instagram post: a picture of herself with her long black hair tied in a pony tail. This was the first time millions of her fans had seen her hair. She also shared a picture of Mahsa and a simple slogan: 'Iranian women are a voice for one another.'[1]

It was a shot in the arm for the movement. It was one thing for veteran critics of the regime to speak out for Mahsa. But this was Katayoun, the staple of Iranian television, the patriarch's smiling daughter-in-law, the wife of Potiphar. If celebrities like her were ready to sacrifice their careers to support the revolution, something big was happening.

Afraid of her courage inspiring others, the regime forces ransacked Riahi's home and took away her belongings. But tipped off in advance, she was able to flee to a village in Qazvin. No one heard from her and many worried about her fate. On 20 November, more than two months later, the security forces finally caught up with the actress.[2] They surrounded her villa in Aybek as if they were arresting a drug lord. The regime media soon boasted about her arrest and charged her with 'publishing false content' and 'helping to sow chaos and disturb public opinion'.

But it was too late by then. Many of Katayoun's peers had already joined her in declaring their support for the movement on the streets. Iran's creatives were up in revolt.

* * *

If Katayoun's act shocked many, few were surprised when another actress, Taraneh Alidsooti, shared a photo of herself without Hijab, holding a sign saying 'Women, Life, Freedom'.[3]

Born in 1984, Taraneh came from a wholly different generation to Katayoun. Too young to remember the bitter days of the 1980s, she grew up when Iran's reformists were in the ascendant. She was only sixteen when she was selected as the lead for what would become a landmark film in Iran: *I'm Taraneh, 15*, the story of a pregnant teenager, divorced from her husband. With its audacious portrayal of women's struggles in Iran brought to life by Taraneh's powerful acting, the film struck a nerve in Iran and beyond. With her debut, Taraneh won a Bronze Leopard at the Locarno International Film Festival and a Crystal Simorgh at the Fajr Film Festival, Iran's most prestigious film awards. Her career went from strength to strength afterwards.

Taraneh came to represent a new age of artists who challenged boundaries, were proud to be politically active and didn't shy away from making demands. She came to identify as a feminist and was a proponent of the #MeToo movement in Iranian cinema. When Donald Trump initiated his Muslim ban in 2017, Taraneh denounced his racism and refused to attend the Oscars, even as *The Salesman,* which she starred in, went on to win the Best International Film prize.

By 2022, Taraneh was no stranger to being in hot water – her consistent public stance against the compulsory Hijab, her open criticism of police violence and her support for political prisoners had turned the regime against her. The police sued her for defamation in 2018. To show her disgust at the status quo, she boycotted Tehran's Fajr festival, which had launched her career over a decade ago.

In June 2022, as the regime was gunning down protesters in Khuzestan, she joined dozens of actors and filmmakers as a signatory to the statement 'Put Your Gun Down', urging security forces not to shoot their fellow Iranians.[4] Two of the signatories, directors Mohammad Rasoulof and Mostafa Ale Ahmad, were thrown in jail. When veteran director Jafar Panahi went to Tehran's Evin prison to inquire about them, they arrested him too.[5] Panahi had been banned from filmmaking for years and had kept skirting the ban by making films clandestinely and sending them to festivals, where he continued to gather awards. Now he was put behind bars – and remains there at the time of writing.

By November, with the street protests well under way, actors and actresses still held back – many threatened with repercussions if they dared to take part. But Taraneh's declaration on 9 November made international headlines. It wasn't a one-off but the opening salvo of a new phase in her activism. Her Instagram page, with over eight million followers, became a new platform for the movement. On 8 December 2022, when a young protester,

Mohsen Shekari, was executed by the regime, Taraneh broadcast an angry message to the authorities: 'Now you will face the consequences of your bloodthirsty action.'[6]

On 17 December, she was finally arrested and sent to Evin, to the gloating of the pro-regime media. 'An actress shouldn't be in prison,' IRGC's *Javan* wrote. 'But if you toy with security, you should expect a proportionate response.'[7]

With one of Iran's best-known actresses in jail, the fury of the film community reached a boiling point. Taraneh was their friend and colleague, not simply a famous name. Many knew that she suffered from severe claustrophobia to the point that she avoided buses. How could she cope in the windowless five-square-metre cells of Evin?

France's union of directors called for her release as did the film festivals of Cannes, Berlin and Locarno. Joining the call were some of the best-known names in world cinema: Kate Winslet, Ken Loach, Jeremy Irons, Pedro Almodóvar, Marion Cotillard and Kristen Stewart.[8]

But more significantly, Iran's own filmmakers and actors started assembling in front of Evin; just like Panahi had a few months ago. But this time, there were too many for the regime to arrest. Taraneh's arrest effectively gave rise to a protest camp on the hills of Evin. Iranian film stars mingled with each other and with families of other protesters. The octogenarian director Bahman Farmanra was visible with his signature brimmed hat covering his bald head. Renowned for spending much of the past few decades in Canadian exile, he was now on the frontline at Evin. At the other end of the political spectrum, you had the clean-shaven actor Shahab Hosseini, who had won Cannes's best actor award when he played alongside Taraneh in *The Salesman*. Not known to be an opponent of the regime by a long shot, he still came to stand up for his colleague. The regime's repression had led to an unlikely event: Iran's film community uniting against it, despite all the risks involved.[9]

After eighteen days in prison, Taraneh was released on bail – a staggering ten billion rials (twenty-two thousand pounds) – on 4 January 2023.[10] Dozens more in the movie industry faced police questioning or arrests.

During the three weeks of her imprisonment, many scenes from Taraneh's films went viral on social media – now shared as support for the new uprising. My favourite was one from the TV series *Shahrzad*. Set in the 1950s, the series features Taraneh as the title character, a medical student who falls in love with Farhad, a left-wing journalist. The series portrays the coup of August 1953, when the Iranian military, colluding with the CIA, MI6 and street toughs they had mobilised, brought down prime minister Mohammad Mossadegh. On the day of the coup, as Farhad is in tears, lamenting the fall of the government and the execution of his comrades, Shahrzad consoles him.

'Wasn't it you who always said that we are passing through a strange phase of history,' Shahrzad says. 'This door will open. This night will end and the sun will rise again. Be patient.'[11]

* * *

Long before the events of autumn 2022, Iranian filmmakers had grown accustomed to working under stringent censorship.

When it came to restrictions on freedom of expression, the Islamic Republic was a world-class champion. In the 2023 World Press Freedom Index of Reporters Without Borders Iran came fourth from last, surpassed only by Vietnam, China and North Korea. But even this ranking doesn't tell the full story. While limitation of political expression is normal in the Middle East and across the authoritarian world, the constraints Iran places on its film industry go far beyond politics.

The compulsory Hijab rule applies to cinema, theatre and TV too. As a result, no woman can ever be portrayed on screen without fully covering her hair, her arms and her legs. Forget kissing or intimate scenes. A woman can never shake a man's hand on screen. A mother can never hug her son on screen. None of this is left to chance. Censors have to approve any film or TV project at every level: from the script to the filming to the final permission for screening. Anybody who has ever worked in this field has stories about the absurd requests censors make – if they weren't real, they'd be laughable.*

In 2018, comedian Amir Mahdi Jule started a new Instagram campaign to publicise how stifling the censors were. With the hashtag #Me_and_The_Censors, the campaign invited artists to

---

* Since both my parents are filmmakers who worked for, or with, the state broadcaster for much of their careers, I grew up on many such absurd stories.

share the most ridiculous demands censors had made. The response was immediate.[12]

Jule kicked it off with his own experiences. He disclosed how the censors had once asked for a scene to be cut from a series because the shape of an actress's ear could be seen from behind the scarf. 'We never understood why they considered the shape of an ear under a scarf to be so arousing,' he quipped. If this sounded improbable, it was quickly confirmed by well-known actress Mitra Hajjar who said she was forced to put plasters on her ears to hide their shape.[13] On another occasion, the censors had said that a woman could not be seen eating a cucumber on screen.[14] An actress had also been told that her teeth shouldn't show when she laughed.[15]

Restrictions weren't limited to women. In 2018, Carles Puyol, FC Barcelona's legendary defender, agreed to come on Iranian TV as an analyst. But he was axed hours before the show because his long hair and many tattoos were thought to be unacceptable.[16] Two years later, as Tehran's popular Persepolis faced off against Qatar's Al Sadd in the AFC Champions League, the Iranian fans were outraged when the live broadcast was cut off in the eighty-ninth minute right after Issa Alekasir scored a header to give Persepolis a 1–0 lead. It turned out that Alekasir had taken his shirt off during his victory lap.[17]

Even animals weren't immune from censorship. A film was once censored because apparently its portrayal of water buffaloes coming out of water, brandishing their behinds, was potentially arousing.[18] When TV was broadcasting a match with AS Roma, it blurred the football club's logo because it showed the teats of a female wolf being sucked on by the mythical founders of the ancient city, Romulus and Remus.[19] And when the Canadian direct-to-video children's film *Against the Wild* was shown on Iranian TV, the censors cut the dogs from it in toto – despite a dog being the third main character. Dogs had recently been prohibited as pets in Iran.[20]

While these were the most ridiculous examples, profound forms of censorship permeated every aspect of the industry. Persian-language poets beloved by millions couldn't be mentioned on TV if they were known to be critical of the regime – ruling out most of them. Iranian directors popular around the world were often unable to show any of their work in the country. Abolfazl Jalili had something of a record in this regard. His *La Gale* (1986), portraying a teenager stuck in a juvenile detention centre, was widely considered a masterpiece and had established him as a major post-revolutionary director. The same was true of his *Det Means Girl* (1994), the story of a rural caretaker who takes his daughter to a city for medical treatment. The film was celebrated in film festivals in Venice, Nantes, Thessaloniki and Tokyo. But even if some of these were screened in Iranian film festivals, none of his fourteen films have ever been allowed to be shown in Iranian cinemas for general audiences.

Now, with some of the leading lights of Iranian cinema arrested or in prison, the industry made a fateful choice – to stand up for itself and throw in its lot with the revolution.

* * *

In joining the movement against the regime, Iranian filmmakers played catch-up to their colleagues in other creative industries. While the film community had suffered from its share of exclusion, censorship and repression, others such as writers, poets, musicians and journalists had long faced harsher restrictions and more extreme persecution.

Ever since its inception, the Islamic Republic was committed to purging the intelligentsia. Even though most of these intellectuals had opposed the Shah and many had initially supported the new regime, Khomeini quickly turned on them. His campaign of fundamentally reshaping Iranian society would not succeed if there were intellectual and creative freedom.

On 8 March 1979, in an address to students in Qom, Khomeini said: 'One shouldn't pick up a pen and write whatever one wants. This would be a betrayal of the nation... This country doesn't belong to those of you who wield your pens. Break your pens. Take refuge in Islam.'[21]

He stubbornly stuck to this message as he consolidated his power. On 17 August 1979, he said: 'We didn't act revolutionarily enough. We ought to have broken the pens of everybody in the press and shut down all corrupt magazine and outlets... We ought to have put up hanging nooses in public squares and exterminated the corrupt and the corrupters.'[22]

Right up to the end of his life in 1989, Khomeini always thought he should have gone further as the predominance of non-Islamists among intellectuals was still evident. Upon his death, some of his most feverish devotees tried to continue his crusade with more extreme methods. Banning them from work no longer sufficed – intellectuals were now physically eliminated.

Most of those targeted were members of the Association of Iranian Writers (AIW). Founded in 1968, AIW had been a thorn in the side of the Shah's regime. In October 1977, it organised a historic series of poetry and essay readings at Tehran's Goethe Institute, playing a pivotal role in the protests leading to the 1979 revolution. The new Islamist regime found this fiercely independent union no less irksome than the Shah did – and it went on to suppress it swiftly and far more thoroughly than the Shah ever attempted. But after Khomeini's death, the regime's methods took a darker turn.

Between 1990 and 1998, dozens of Iranian intellectuals, most of them AIW members, were mysteriously murdered. Some had seemingly died in car accidents. Bodies had been mutilated by knives. Others died of heart attacks that were later found to be a result of injecting potassium into their veins. In 1996, a remarkable plan on the life of dozens of writers failed only at the last moment. High-ranking AIW members had been invited on a cultural trip to the neighbouring Armenia. Since they were very few flights from Tehran to Yerevan, a bus trip was organised. Twenty one writers, the best and brightest of Iran's intellectual community, signed up to go. The bus had reached the snaking mountain roads of northern Iran when the writers realised that the driver had jumped out and the bus was about to descend precipitously into a valley. Only a last-minute intervention by novelist Shahriyar Mandanipour saved everybody's lives. Better known for his postmodernist novels than daredevil driving skills, Mandanipour grabbed the handbrake before the bus went into freefall.[23] But this wasn't the end of regime's murderous campaign against the intellectuals.

Following the election of reformist Khatami to presidency in 1997, the pace of killings quickened. It was later revealed that elements inside the regime establishment and its Ministry of Intelligence had masterminded the attacks and had wanted to use them to undermine Khatami. In November and December 1998, within the space of a few weeks, several high profile murders appalled the nation. On 22 November, Dariosh Forohar and his wife, Parvane Eskandari, old-school left-leaning liberals, were killed in their home in a brutal knife attack; Parvane's breasts had been cut off.[24] Some weeks later, two well-known writers were also murdered: Mohammad Mokhtari, a leftist known for his translations of Russian poets such as Anna Akhmatova and Vladimir Mayakovsky, and Mohammad Jafar Pooyandeh, the translator of the Universal Declaration of Human Rights.

But the killers had badly miscalculated the public mood. Instead of undermining Khatami, the murders sparked a public campaign for accountability. Soon christened the 'Chain Murders', the anti-intellectual atrocities became a burning political issue and key to the conflict between supporters and opponents of reform. When it became clear the murders originated in the Ministry of Intelligence, Khatami fired the minister. A trial was finally held but the main defendant, an old agent of the Ministry of Intelligence named Saeed Emami, was found dead in his cell in

June 1999. According to the authorities, he had committed suicide by drinking a depilatory. At the same time, journalists asking questions about these murders were arrested. The conservative judiciary didn't hesitate to shut down the reformist media outlets who broke the story when it had its chance in 2000.

While the writers didn't quite win against the establishment, they did not surrender. In 2008, AIW declared 4 December, a date that fell between the murders of Mokhtari and Pooyandeh, as the Day of Combatting Censorship.[25] The association intended to organise a large gathering in the cemetery near Tehran where Mokhtari and Pooyandeh were buried. But the authorities had blocked this from happening.

This didn't stop AIW. Speaking to the press, left-wing lawyer Nasser Zarafshan announced the establishment of AIW's Anti-Censorship Committee. Zarafshan represented the families of the Chain Murders victims. Pointing out that censorship in Iran had been a constant through Qajar, Pahlavi and the Islamic Republic regimes, he said that the new committee wasn't the preserve of the ivory tower; it belonged to the people.

'When we speak of censorship, this isn't just about books and the press,' he said. 'When we speak of the freedom of conscience and expression, this is a much broader issue and its victims are not just writers, translators and publishers. It includes other artistic fields such as cinema, theatre, the press... We want to bring together all the professions and social forces who have a stake here.'[26]

* * *

Over the years, the regime did everything it could to disrupt AIW. If a few members tried to meet in somebody's house to hold elections, the regime forces would find out and raid the meeting. In order to survive, members held elections by postal ballot and met in small groups in cafes or bookshops to elude regime surveillance.

The association never gave up and a new generation of writers flocked to its banner. One was Bektash Abtin, a poet known for his innovative use of free verse. Born in late 1974 in a religious family near Tehran, Abtin's life, like so many of his peers, had been shaped by the Iran–Iraq War. His father was a survivor of Saddam's chemical attacks and a maternal uncle had been killed in the war in 1983. In his young years, he had been a member of IRGC's volunteer force, the Basij, and had tried to alter his ID card to appear older and serve in the war.

But, like many of his generation, his attitudes changed in the post-war years of 1990s. When he finally did his military service, he discovered a new passion for modern Persian poetry. Changing his birth name from the average-sounding Mehdi Kazemi to the more poetic Bektash Abtin, he quickly became a fixture in Iran's poetry scene. In 2011, his fourth poetry book, *The Hammer*, won a top award. Also dabbling in filmmaking, his documentary about Loris Tjeknavorian, the noted Iranian-Armenian composer, gave him another trophy for his cabinet in 2012.

Amid all the accolades, much of his life revolved around AIW which he joined in 2010. Like many other Iranians, he had taken part in the Green Movement protests of 2009 and was injured by the security forces. In the aftermath, he searched for a vehicle of activity and he found it in AIW. As he'd later say: 'The AIW gave me an identity. It taught me what freedom was. It taught me why we gather together; what do we speak about? What is it that we want?'[27]

Soon elected to the leadership of AIW, he reaped the benefits of the job: prosecution and jail. In 2020 he was tried on charges of 'Propaganda against the regime', 'Gathering and collusion aimed at acting against national security' and 'Encouraging Iranian women to prostitution and corruption'. The latter seemed to be based on a satirical poem in which he depicted a prostitute. He was sentenced to six years in prison by the Revolutionary Courts.

A big bulky man, Abtin suffered from a number of conditions aggravated by the conditions in Evin. To make things worse, he contracted Covid-19 twice. Denying medical care had long been a weapon in the arsenal of the regime. Despite repeated pleas by so many of his peers, Abtin was not released or given proper care, even as his health deteriorated. In July 2021, he was briefly taken to a hospital but pictures soon circulated that showed his feet in shackles, chained to the hospital bed. It led to such a wave of outrage that even the judiciary's chief complained and asked: 'When someone hasn't committed a violent crime, he shouldn't be shackled. Is he an ISIS member or a terrorist to be shackled?' The authorities claimed that those who had mistreated Abtin would be punished. Yet he was still refused proper treatment and, on a second visit to hospital, was shackled again. By the autumn, his condition had worsened dramatically. AIW warned that his life was in serious danger. On 8 January 2022, their fears were realised. Bektash Abtin died in Tehran's Sassan hospital.

At first, the regime tried to deny him even the dignity of a burial. But as messages of anger and protest flooded in from around the world, they had to relent and the family was finally able to hold a funeral in Shahr-e Rey, where he was born. The event became a gathering of writers and other creatives. Jafar Panahi could be seen in the crowds. Many chanted 'Salute to Abtin, Death to the tyrants', 'Death to the murderous regime' and 'Death to the dictator'. Vigils were held in his honour in Paris, Brussels, Hamburg, Cologne, Vancouver and Los Angeles. More sombrely, on 10 January, his fellow prisoners in Evin held an hour-long vigil and a courageous protest in the courtyard.

On the surface, there was very little hope in the story of Abtin's brutal death. Once more, Iranian writers had been forced to bury one of their own. Once more a writer had become a martyr. But the indignation quickly spreading among writers, and the public sympathy that the struggle for Abtin's health and freedom had garnered proved that Iran's intellectuals were still up and fighting – despite every effort by the regime to quash them.

When the uprisings of September 2022 began, Abtin's unjust death still stung like a fresh wound. With no hesitation, writers, artists and intellectuals joined the revolution, ready to take action. On 23 September, the AIW issued a thundering call, asking all writers and artists to 'reject the conventional seeking of safe harbours and openly support the freedom movement of the people'. The movement, it said, 'was result of an anger that is forty years old'. The statement dripped with unprecedented rage.[28]

The writers, many of whom were fighting on the streets alongside others, were prepared to go even further. On 21 November, 250 translators pledged solidarity with the movement. They promised to defy censorship by publishing uncensored translations that had been prohibited by the regime, in any way possible. With a touch of humility, they added: 'We are aware that this ray of light would pale next to the shining sun of this movement and its youth.'[29]

A few days later, more than sixty writers issued a similar statement with a similar pledge. 'We promise ourselves and our readers to publish our works without censorship, by any means necessary,' read the statement, drafted by the Iranian-Canadian author Fereshte Molavi. 'We don't want to be ashamed before the history, culture and literature of Iran and before our readers. We, the people of letters, testify that we are aware of our rights and will commit to playing our part in building the future of Iran.'[30]

The statement drew attention to two European writers who, separated by a century, represented the best intellectual traditions that Iranian writers now identified themselves with.

'We, the people of letters, know that Emile Zola stood up all alone to speak of a truth that no obstacle could ever stop,' the statement said. 'We know that Vaclav Havel wrote his *Living in Truth* to open a path to a bright future. We know that in our yesterday and today, we've had and continue to have poets and writers who have lost their lives on the path of freedom, truth and justice.'

The reference to the Czech Havel, long a favourite of Eastern Europe-obsessed Iranians, was expected. But why draw upon a French writer from the nineteenth century?

In 1890s, Zola had found himself faced with the Dreyfus Affair – the conviction of a Jewish French artillery officer and his imprisonment on Devil's Island in French Guiana; an antisemitic scandal that divided the French Republic. In response, novelist Zola had penned an unparalleled masterpiece: an open letter, headlined *J'Accuse...!* Convicted of libel, Zola had had to flee to England to escape prison but the power of his words reverberated through time and place. In 1923, when a Mexican MP gave a speech against an American ambassador, he used the term *J'Accuse.* In 1925, when the Arab Palestinian newspaper *Filastin* published an editorial against the Balfour Declaration, it used the phrase *J'Accuse.* Zola's name now stood for a belief that a writer's pen should indict the perpetrators of injustice.

In 2022, the Iranian writers didn't need to say the word. They hadn't even needed to mention Zola. Together with filmmakers, poets, translators and the rest of Iranians, their valiant defiance of censorship was a momentous *J'accuse* that the regime could not shake off. After forty-three years of trying, their pens had still not been broken.

Six

We Are All Iranians: The Fight for Freedom of Religion

When protests broke out in Iran following Mahsa's death on 16 September 2023, it soon became clear that this represented the most serious challenge to the regime since 2009. But how far would this new movement spread?

Previous waves of protest hadn't always translated well across all of Iran. The 2009 Green Movement was centred around Tehran and other major cities in central Iran like Isfahan. It failed to enthuse large numbers in Azeri- and Kurdish-majority areas of western Iran. The 2019 protests and strikes mobilised many workers in Iran's more peripheral provinces, yet Iran's urban middle class in cities like Tehran remained largely indifferent. But in 2022, the movement seemed to touch every corner of Iran. It had started with the killing of a Kurdish girl in Tehran and had quickly spread to her hometown and other Kurdish-majority cities in western Iran as well as other major cities such as Rasht and Isfahan. But would it flourish everywhere? Where would be the next big epicentre?

Thousands of kilometres away from Kurdistan, on the opposite side of the country, lies the southeastern Sistan and Balochistan, Iran's second biggest province and its poorest. It's distinguished by the Martian mountains, idyllic beaches and strategic import – its immediate neighbours are Afghanistan, Pakistan and the Gulf of Oman. Like most provinces on the Iranian borders, its inhabitants' mother tongue differs from the country's only official language, Persian. They speak Balochi, like their fellow Baloch in the neighbouring province in Pakistan. But it stands apart from much of Iran in one further crucial respect. Like Kurdistan, most of its people are Sunni Muslims, belonging to Iran's largest religious minority.

While more than 90% of Iranians are Shia Muslims, from 8–10% belong to the Sunni branch of Islam. The remaining 1–2% are Bahá'ís, Zoroastrians, Christians, Jews and believers in other faiths, although these demographic statistics only record religion at birth, not belief itself. Many Iranian young people are atheistic or agnostic but this would never be officially declared as the Islamic Republic could subject them to the death penalty. This grisly fate also awaits those who convert out of Islam or even from Shia Islam to another branch – both acts of apostasy. Bahman Shakoori, a Shia man who became a Sunni, suffered such a fate as one of the first victims of the Republic's apostasy laws. He was convicted of 'insulting Prophet Muhammad' because, like many Sunnis, he had criticised the prevalent Shia custom of paying pilgrimage to the graves of Muslim saints. In autumn 1980, the Republic executed him.[1] Iranian Sunnis jarred with the Islamic Republic's ideal of a state governed by Shia Islam from the very beginning.

The Baloch people, already on the economic margins, also faced religious oppression. They had every reason to revolt. As the Women, Life, Freedom movement spread around the country like wildfire, the Baloch had their own grievances, and they were ready to be heard.

Weeks before Mahsa's killing in Tehran, a fifteen-year-old Baloch girl had suffered mistreatment at the hands of the authorities. She hailed from the Dashtyari, Iran's southerneastmost county, right next to the port of Chabahar, vital for Indian Ocean trade. On 1 September, she was taken in for interrogation by the police commander of Chabahar when, according to the Baloch Activists Campaign, she was raped. It took time for the news to spread and many of the locals were reluctant to share it, out of consideration for the girl's privacy. But on 27 September, Abdolqafar Naqshbandi, the Imam for the Friday prayers in the nearby city of Rask, confirmed the news and called for a public trial of the police chief, who was allegedly a rapist.[2] The whole province seethed in anger. In Chabahar, young people burnt buildings down that very night. But the real show of force was yet to come – on Friday, when everyone would gather for the congregational prayer in the mosques.

On 30 September, Friday prayers in the provincial centre of Zahedan were led by Maulavi Abdulhamid, the top Sunni cleric of Iran since 1987. Sitting on his throne-like wooden seat, Abdulhamid cut a familiar figure, with his bushy grey beard, white turban and twitching eyes.[3] In the khutba, the sermon given before the prayer, he spoke with a calm and measured tone and a smile and patiently counselled officials. He spoke of how Prophet Muhammad had liked to hear criticism, even from ordinary people. The implicit contrast was with the regime's rulers, who preferred to answer criticism with bullets. He called for a 'series of changes' in the country so that it could de-escalate regional tensions and improve the livelihood of its people. Echoing a popular theme with the protesters, he spoke of how rich Iran was in 'talent and wealth' and lamented that all this was being squandered. Addressing the police and security forces, he gently asked them to be more 'tolerant' of people. All in all, it was hardly a rabblerousing speech of a revolutionary firebrand.

As the congregational prayers wrapped up, a group of people headed toward a nearby police station. They wanted to protest the police chief's rape of a fifteen-year-old girl with total impunity and declare their solidarity with the Women, Life, Freedom movement. Although a minority threw stones at the station, it was by and large a peaceful gathering. No one could have predicted what would happen next.

Special security units had already been installed inside the police station and unmarked snipers perched on the roofs of nearby buildings. Suddenly they started shooting at protesters from all directions, as video coverage documents. They didn't stop at just dispersing the demonstration. Plainclothes and uniformed officers descended onto the shops and malls where protesters sought refuge. Dozens more were shot within an hour. Helicopters circled above the bloodied centre of Zahedan, creating an air of a pre-planned event.

By the evening of 30 September, it was clear that the regime had committed a gruesome crime, the worst since the nationwide uprising began. The authorities hastened to claim that the violence was instigated by an armed attack by Jaish ul-Adl, a Sunni jihadist group designated as terrorists by both Iran and the US. But the group had been barely active for years and no one bought the regime's habitual deflections. The Baloch rights group quickly started publishing the long list of dozens who had been killed in what we now call the Black Friday of 2022 or the Zahedan massacre.

Iranians around the country, most of whom had never visited Sistan and Balochistan, were shaken to see their fellow citizens rising up with such valour. As the list of martyrs grew, so too did their reach on social media – their pictures and stories plastered all over Facebook, Instagram and Twitter timelines. The death toll in Zahedan ultimately reached ninety-six protesters.

Khodanoor Lojei's story particularly captured the imagination of ordinary Iranians. He was twenty-six years old at the time of the protests. Khodanoor, whose name means Light of God in Persian, lived in an immiserated district of Zahedan, Shirabad. Its conditions exemplified the decades of neglect imposed upon the province: homes didn't have piped water, most roads were not paved and most people lived in poverty. Many like Khodanoor didn't even have basic identity documents and were essentially stateless. But Khodanoor had still made a good life for himself. By day, he worked as a cement labourer. But outside of that, he had an Instagram account with thousands of followers, where he introduced people to Baloch music through his energetic dancing.

Like many of the Baloch youth, Khodanoor had seen the inside of a prison before. According to his family, he had a dispute with the son of a local official, who then probably bribed someone to get him arrested. A photograph of Khodanoor handcuffed to a flagpole went viral. Having been released on bail a few weeks before, he joined his fellow Zahedanis in the protests of 30 September. When snipers shot into the crowds, Khodanoor was hit in the kidney. He begged for treatment in the hospital. He told the doctors and nurses that his mother and his eight sisters relied on him. Yet proper care was not forthcoming and on 2 October, the day of his twenty-seventh birthday, he passed away. One of his sisters suffered a fatal heart attack when she heard of his death.

* * *

The regime had long hoped to rely on religious and ethnic differences amongst Iranians to divide them. To many a Tehrani,

Balochistan was a distant land of peoples with different customs, notorious for its drug smuggling routes, tribal honour codes and Salafi-jihadist groups. Would they show solidarity for the Baloch?

The regime's ferocious attack on Balochistan put it on the map of the nationwide protest movement. The stories of Khodanoor and the other martyrs of the Zahedan massacre spread quickly. Protesters shouted chants such as: 'Khodanoor has been killed by a bunch of mercenaries.' Almost immediately, a new slogan circulated throughout the country and beyond: 'From Zahedan to Tehran, I give my life for Iran.' Different versions connected Zahedan to Kurdistan, Azerbaijan and other parts of the country. In the throes of a popular movement, the nation was being born anew.

To commemorate him, supporters from Tabriz to Montreal replicated the haunting image of Khodanoor handcuffed to a flagpole, evocative of traditional Iranian revolutionary romanticism. A futsal player in the neighbouring Kerman province replicated the gesture as his goal celebration, broadcast live to thousands.[4] In front of Chicago's Art Institute, Iranian activists unveiled an illuminated ice sculpture of him. But he was not only memorialised as a martyr, but as someone with a joy for life.[5] In Tehran's iconic Azadi Square, a Baloch girl donned a beautifully embroidered red and blue traditional dress and performed one of his most popular Instagram dances. The revolution had found a new beating heart.

Bloody Friday did not deter the Baloch from resisting the regime. For weeks on end, every Friday prayer in Zahedan was followed by mass demonstrations. Protesters chanted Persian-language slogans such as 'Death to Khamenei' and 'Death to the dictator' in solidarity with the national movement, but they also threw the spotlight on issues they faced in Balochistan: severe poverty which made Sistan and Balochistan the poorest province in the country; lack of proper schools, potable water and other public services in this distant, mainly rural province; 40% unemployment; and the statelessness faced by tens of thousands of Baloch who had lived in Iran for generations but didn't have the right paperwork.

These protesters had something the rest of Iran still lacked: a recognised political leader in Maulavi Abdulhamid. Although Khamenei's regime was no stranger to imprisoning and assassinating any threats to their power, they had never been able to get rid of Abdulhamid.

Born in a small village in Balochistan in 1947, Abdulhamid had pursed religious education in the neighbouring Sunni-majority Pakistan. He had studied in seminaries all over the country, including under Abdulghani Jajravi, a legendary scholar of tafsir and hadith, who built his own school in Punjab. While burnishing his scholarly credentials, Abdulhamid also made smart political moves that testified to his ambition. Upon his return to Iran in the 1970s, he married the daughter of Iran's then top Sunni cleric, Abdolaziz Molazadeh. In the early 1970s, Molazadeh had built two major religious institutions in Zahedan, cementing his leadership in the community. The centrepiece of this effort was the Grand Makki Mosque in Zahedan. With its

Ottoman-style architecture, four large minarets and cascading cupolas, the mosque would have looked at home in Istanbul or Bursa. This was deliberate – it had been designed after Istanbul's fabled Blue Mosque and the Prophet's Mosque in Medina. At the heart of a Sunni-majority city in a Shia-majority country, the mosque epitomised the growing confidence of the Sunni community. Right next to it was the Zahedan Seminary, Iran's largest religious school for Sunnis, also ran by Molazadeh. It had started life as a tiny institution with a few dozen students and six teachers, including Abdulhamid. It soon boasted hundreds of students and a Sunni-focused library unique in Iran.

When the 1979 revolution broke out, Molazadeh was among the leaders of minority religious communities able to keep their positions in the post-revolutionary era. He was elected to the Constitutional Assembly and remained in charge of Zahedan's grand mosque. He had passed on the leadership of the seminary to his son-in-law, Abdulhamid, in 1977 on account of poor health. In 1987, when Molazadeh passed away, Abdulhamid also took over the mosque. More importantly, he succeeded Molazadeh as the Imam of the Friday prayer in Zahedan, meaning he led the congregation. In the footsteps of his father-in-law, Abdulhamid now controlled all three top jobs of Iran's most important Sunni community.

By the time of the Zahedan protests of 2022, Abdulhamid was one of the very few officials who had been at the helm for longer than Khamenei himself. Throughout the years, he had perfected a balancing act in which he pushed for rights and liberties for the

Iranian Baloch and other Sunni communities while also assert-
ing his support for Shia–Sunni friendship and Iran's territorial
integrity. He was both widely admired in his community and
respected as a communal leader by Tehran. He had amassed
enough power that even Khamenei knew he couldn't be touched
without risking a massive upheaval. Abdulhamid knew this too
and was unafraid of directly criticising Khamenei, unlike many
other religious leaders. In a fiery speech in 2009, he said: 'Why
should those appointed by the Supreme Leader decide what's
best for Sunnis? Sunnis decide Sunni affairs.'[6]

He consistently advocated for the Sunni community's rights,
fearing no repercussions. Why were the Sunnis not allowed to
observe their religious ceremonies, especially in places like
Tehran or Isfahan when they were in the minority? Why did
Tehran not have a Sunni mosque despite having hundreds of
thousands of Sunnis? Not afraid to call the constitution into
question, Abdulhamid decried its policy of reserving top positions such as the Supreme Leader and president for Iranian Shias.

He also built himself up as a national figure admired by
reformers as open-minded and liberal-leaning. He opposed the
use of capital punishment, which was disproportionately used in
Sunni-majority areas like Balochistan and Kurdistan. He pushed
for ecumenicalism and was always the first in decrying the acts of
anti-Shia hatred incited by Sunni Islamists in the region. In 2013,
when an Al Qaeda affiliate destroyed a Shia shrine in Syria,
Abdulhamid swiftly condemned it.[7] In 2014, Defenders of
Human Rights Center (DHRC), co-founded by Nobel laureate

Shirin Ebadi, awarded him its annual human rights award for 'establishing peaceful relations between a variety of ethnicities and religious tendencies in Sistan and Balochistan province'.[8]

Some of his positions, undoubtedly pursued for cynical reasons, were far more questionable. His unfounded claim that the Covid-19 pandemic had spread in Iran due to the presence of Chinese clerical students in Qom was a thinly-veiled attempt at riding the Sinophobic wave in the country.[9] As the Iranian regime warmed to the Taliban returning to power in next-door Afghanistan, Abdulhamid's praise for the group, aligning him with the Tehran hardliners, enraged more liberal and secular Iranians. The DHRC took back its award in 2021 in protest.[10] In the same year, Abdulhamid endorsed Khamenei's favourite presidential candidate, Ebrahim Raisi, in exchange for being promised better rights for Sunnis.[11]

But as Zahedan became the centre stage for the national revolt, Abdulhamid's keen political instincts told him the time was up for his decades-long balancing act between currying favour with the regime and advocating for the Sunni community. Following the massacre on 30 September, he grew increasingly bold. He publicly rejected the authorities' sham allegations of armed demonstrators. He asserted that the protesters had been peaceful – the snipers and plainclothes officers had shot at them. Most significantly, he pinned the blame directly on Khamenei.

In his next week Friday sermon, on 7 October, he described the massacre at length and exalted those killed as martyrs. He contended that the majority of the victims had been shot directly in the head and the chest: the shooters had aimed to kill. He also revealed that the regime had sent people to negotiate with him directly, perhaps hoping that he would call the protests off or change his version of events. But he had told them exactly what he was telling people now.[12]

Abdulhamid's pulpit in Zahedan now became a call to the people. Iranians were used to imams spouting out Khamenei's line in the sermons before Friday prayers. But in this southeastern corner of Iran, Abdulhamid's weekly sermon went directly against the regime. On 4 November, he argued that the majority of Iranians were unhappy with the status quo and added: 'If you don't believe it, hold a referendum with international observers and accept the results.'[13]

'For fifty days now, this nation is coming onto the streets to protest,' Abdulhamid said defiantly. 'You can't push them back by killing them, beating them up or putting them in prison.' He once more commemorated the Zahedan massacre victims and suggested they were martyrs for the whole of the Iranian nation, and had made similar sacrifices: 'In a few hours, the number of our killed equalled those of all the rest of Iran.'

On 2 December, Abdulhamid called for the release of all the protesters and said: 'We want our country to be united... This shouldn't be about Shia or Sunni, or this or that ethnicity. We are all Iranians. Including Zoroastrians, Sufi Dervishes and followers of all religions, even the Bahá'ís. Bahá'ís are also human beings. They belong to Iran, they have rights and these rights must be observed.'[14]

With a simple statement, Abdulhamid had broken a longstanding taboo. Reform-minded religious leaders never dared to broach the question of Bahá'í rights – a minority so persecuted its members could not even attend university. Few publicly questioned the regime narrative of the Bahá'í faith not being a real religion.

As the leader of Iran's largest religious minority, Abdulhamid had come to the defence of its largest non-Muslim minority. Encouraged by the positive reception, Abdulhamid reaffirmed his message on 30 December: 'We have Jews, Christians and also Bahá'ís. They are all entitled to human rights and citizenship rights. Even those who don't believe in the God are entitled to human rights.'[15]

He was met with a swift reaction on both sides. As revolutionaries and reformers praised Abdulhamid for his historic move, the regime outlets rained attacks on him. *Tasnim*, a news agency close to the IRGC, brayed that he had 'violated both Islamic jurisprudence and national security'. It claimed that Bahá'ís were 'not a religion but a political and espionage organisation.'[16] Other pieces by pro-regime outlets cited years-old criticisms of Bahá'ís from Sunni authorities, such as sheikhs of Egypt's al-Azhar, the prominent Syrian scholar Rashid Rida and pro-regime Sunni clerics from western Iran.[17] This was all from the regime's usual playbook in times of crisis: pitting one minority against another. Yet if Sunnis were marginalised under the regime, the Bahá'ís were being hunted into non-existence.

* * *

Ever since it started life in Iran in the 1840s, the Bahá'í faith has faced varying degrees of persecution in the country. Under both the Qajar and Pahlavi dynasties, they faced legal discrimination and occasional pogroms following Shia clerics inciting their followers. Many of the faith's tenets threatened the Shia religious establishment. Opposed to an entrenched clerical class, Bahá'ís were instead guided by local and national 'spiritual assemblies' elected by the faithful via secret ballots. They advocated gender equality and opposed forced veiling for women. They insisted on unity of all people (or 'oneness of humanity' as Bahá'ís like to call it) and had a sympathetic attitude to traditions and holy books of Islam, Judaism, Christianity, Buddhism and other faiths.

Bahá'ís date their faith to the messianic claims of Shiraz-born Seyyed Ali Mohammad Shirazi, known to his followers as the Bab (Arabic for 'Gate') who was executed in 1850. The Bab's mantle was picked up by a follower who adopted the name Baha'u'llah (Arabic for 'Glory of God') and founded the Bahá'í faith. Baha'u'llah was exiled from Iran in 1853 and experienced banishment throughout the Ottoman Empire from Baghdad to Adrianople (Edirne). In 1868, collusion between Tehran and Constantinople resulted in his incarceration in a medieval castle in Acre, Ottoman Palestine, where he spent the last few decades of his life. Yet despite these unpromising beginnings, the faith quickly took off in the second half of the nineteenth century. Throughout the twentieth century, it found millions of followers in every single country in the world, making it the second most widespread religion in the world after Christianity. But nothing could prepare it for the persecution it would face in Iran once again after the 1979 revolution. As early as the 1960s, the revolution's leader, Khomeini, declared Bahá'ís to be *kuffar* (unbelievers) and *najis* (ritually unclean), accusing them of being behind dangerous reforms like female suffrage. He called on his followers to ostracise Bahá'ís. Anti-Bahá'í ideas also relied on concocted stories similar to Judeo-Masonic conspiracies that had energised European fascism a few short decades ago. The fact that the faith's headquarters were in Haifa resulted in baseless theories about their alleged Zionist links. In fact, the faith's base in Israel was a mere accident of history, as Baha'u'llah was buried in what was then Ottoman Palestine. In reality, Bahá'ís were known to be scrupulously observant of laws in Iran, as in any other country, and averse to political participation. None of the long list of conspiracies about their alleged collaboration with Britain, the Soviet Union, Israel or the US contain a grain of truth.

But upon the establishment of the Islamic Republic in 1979, this anti-Bahá'í attitude was enshrined into state policy. At the outset, the regime's constitution recognised three non-Muslim minorities – Christians, Jews and Zoroastrians – and accorded them parliamentary representation. While these communities continued to face discrimination, the lot of Iranian Bahá'ís was invariably worse. They were to now be among Iran's most persecuted citizens.

On 21 August 1980, IRGC forces raided a meeting of the National Spiritual Assembly held at a member's private home. The nine elected members of the body, alongside two other present Bahá'ís, were arrested without a warrant.[18] In a meeting with their families, a key figure of the regime, Akbar Hashemi Rafsanjani, confirmed that they had been arrested. But he later went back on his word and said he didn't know who had arrested the eleven Bahá'ís or where they were being held.[19] At the time of writing, the fate of these eleven Bahá'ís has never been disclosed. Subsequently, the nine people elected to form the new National Spiritual Assembly of Bahá'ís were executed without trial on 27 December 1981.[20] The regime claimed, without a shred of evidence, that they had been spying for foreign countries. More than two hundred Bahá'ís were killed in the early years of the Islamic Republic.

More insidiously, the regime continued a persistent policy of socially marginalising Bahá'ís. In 1991, the Supreme Council of Cultural Revolution issued a secret circular, altering the lives of hundreds of thousands of Bahá'ís in the Islamic Republic. They were not to be deported, imprisoned or punished 'without reason'. Instead, 'the regime should work so that the path to their progress is blocked.'[21] A cornerstone of this deliberate policy of subjugation was a strict ban on Bahá'ís entering universities, and for all currently enrolled Bahá'ís to be expelled. The regime also deliberately impoverished Bahá'ís by excluding them from a variety of jobs and professions. If a shop was found shut on Bahá'í holidays, the authorities could close it down. If a civil servant was discovered to be a Bahá'í, he could lose his job. Bahá'ís were often barred from selling land or even keeping titles to the lands they had owned for decades. The Bahá'í International

Community soon found an apt name for this state of affairs: economic apartheid.[22] During the long years of apartheid, South African Bahá'ís of all colours had resisted segregation by holding integrated meetings, just as they had in the American South. They now asked the world to support them in their struggle in Iran.[23]

Bahá'ís also resisted in their own unique ways. In 1987, they established the Bahá'í Institute for Higher Education, a clandestine university that served the Iranian Bahá'ís who were otherwise deprived from education. The advent of the internet allowed the BIHE to expand, as it could now employ professors from around the world. Organising classes in hundreds of living rooms around the country, BIHE now offers diplomas, bachelors and master's degrees in a variety of fields, from civil engineering to architecture, from Persian language to music. More than eighty universities around the world have entered into agreements with BIHE, accrediting its degrees.

But, as the case of Maulavi Abdulhamid shows, defence of Bahá'í rights has not been limited to Bahá'ís. Disgusted with their government's campaign against their compatriots, many non-Bahá'í Iranians have risen to their defence, despite the risk of experiencing persecution by the regime. In 2014, documentary filmmaker and journalist Maziar Bahari launched an international campaign called Education is Not a Crime, highlighting the astonishing achievements of BIHE and painting murals around the world about Bahá'ís who defied the restrictions to seek education at all costs.

Meanwhile, in Iran's prison cells, as Bahá'ís were jailed along-side their fellow Iranians of all faiths, new bonds of solidarity formed. One such bond arose between two unlikely candidates. Fariba Kamal-Abadi had been arrested in 2008, alongside six fellow Bahá'í community leaders, collectively known as the Bahá'í Seven. Sentenced to long years in prison, she came to share a cell with generations of Iranian political prisoners. In 2013, a new prisoner was added to the block: Faeze Hashemi Rafsanjani, a former Tehran MP and daughter of a former president, Akbar Hashemi Rafsanjani, the same man who had once denied the regime's role in the disappearance of the Bahá'í leaders. On the face of it, Fariba and Faeze couldn't be more different. One hailed from an elite family of Iranian politicians; the other had to live as a second-class citizen in her own country. But with the regime now expanding the circle of exclusion, they both found themselves in Evin. Both born in early 1960s, they soon struck up a friendship.

In May 2016, Fariba was released on furlough, her first time outside of Evin in eight years. Having been released earlier, Faeze decided on what was at once a simple yet historic move. She visited Fariba and her family at their house.[24] It was an act of courtesy, familiar to Iranians who liked to pay calls to each other in times of trouble. Prepared to pay the high price of fraternising with a Bahá'í, Faeze allowed a picture to be published of the meeting. Here she was, in her long black chador, sitting next to Fariba and a number of her relatives, many of them women with unveiled hair, all under a picture of Abdulbaha, Baha'u'llah's son and successor.

The picture was like a red flag to the bulls of the regime. The daughter of an ayatollah was hobnobbing with Baháʼís under a picture of one of their religious leaders. Dozens of pro-regime outlets and personalities initiated immediate attacks. A cleric from the Assembly of Experts called Faeze a 'traitor to Islam and the revolution'. Ayatollah Makarem Shirazi, a leading Shia authority, attacked her for having met 'Baháʼís who are agents of the US and Israel'.[25] Even her supportive father reprimanded her and condemned the Baháʼí faith as deviant and harmful.[26] But Faeze stood her ground and defended the visit.

'I went to see Ms Kamalabadi because she was my cellmate and we lived together for six months,' Faeze told Euronews in an interview.[27] 'After eight years, she had five days outside prison. This was a very ordinary meeting. We are not animals. As humans, we have ethical and humane duties... in Iran, nobody is oppressed like the Baháʼís.'

If anyone needed a sign of changing times, this was it. By 2021, when the Baháʼís launched an initiative online to counter the state-sponsored campaign of hate, no one was surprised that many prominent Iranians joined. Using the hashtag #StopHatePropaganda, the campaign encouraged individual Baháʼís to share their stories of discrimination while non-Baháʼís pledged their support for equality. Activist Narges Mohmmadi, actress Mahnaz Afshar and historian Abbas Milani were among the many who joined.[28]

'The terrible wall of silence is breaking,' Milani said.

* * *

Sunnis and Bahá'ís are the two largest communities to suffer from religious discrimination in Iran. Followers of other religions not recognised in the constitution such as the Yarsan, Hindus, Buddhists and Sikhs are also deprived from many basic rights. Like Bahá'ís, they are barred from government jobs. And even the two other Abrahamic religions whose followers are recognised as People of the Book by the regime are subject to oppression.

No non-Muslim has ever become a minister, a deputy minister or even department head in the Islamic Republic. In 2017, Sepanta Niknam, a Zoroastrian city councillor in Yazd, was kicked off the council despite having won the elections, explicitly because he was non-Muslim. He was only restored by an order of the Expediency Council in 2018 after widespread outrage.[29] When he tried to run for the Tehran City Council in 2021, he was turned down, once more explicitly because he wasn't a Muslim.[30] Practising a millennia-old religion that had been the faith of a majority of Iranians prior to the advent of Islam, the small Zoroastrian community now faces many restrictions in its home country. Authorities regularly stop public celebrations of ancient Iranian festivals such as the Zoroastrian Sadeh.[31] Zoroastrian students are frequently disciplined if they display any signs of their religion like a Zoroastrian calendar or a Fravashi necklace.[32] Iranian Jews, whose roots in the country goes back to more than two thousand years, constitute the biggest Jewish population in the Middle East outside Israel. But their population has dwindled to around ten thousand, which is less than one-tenth of its size in 1979. The Iranian regime's anti-Israeli campaign has long used antisemitic motifs, including Holocaust denial. Khamenei remains the only head of state in the world to actively and repeatedly deny the murder of six million Jews by Nazi Germany.[33] Among Christians, while traditional communities such as Armenians, Assyrians and Chaldeans are tolerated, new converts and home churches are actively repressed. The punishment for apostasy remains a constant threat for the growing community of Christian converts.

But just as the regime ploughs ahead with its campaign of religious repression, Iranian society has never been more open to religious diversity. While shops that brandish the ancient Zoroastrian symbol Fravashi are closed down, Iranians of all faiths embrace this symbol as part of an ancient national culture. The antisemitic and anti-Bahá'í campaigns of the ruling Islamists had once carried some weight with parts of the intellectual class. Now most Iranians reject these claims as propaganda.

In December 2022, when Maulavi Abdulhamid declared, 'We are all Iranians', he spoke for a new nation in the making. A Sunni cleric now became a figurehead for an Iranian revolution. In the long decades since 1979 instituted a Shia theocracy in Iran, something had changed. Religious freedom was now the order of the day.

Seven

Our Common Pain: The Fight for Refugee Rights

The cry 'Women, Life, Freedom' spread like wildfire across the world in autumn 2022. But in one nation, the declarations of solidarity cut deeper, their assertion of camaraderie felt more immediate than any other: Afghanistan.

Alongside Iran and Tajikistan, Afghanistan is one of the only three countries in the world whose official language is Persian, termed Dari by the Afghan government since 1964. Cultural and linguistic ties connect millions across the 921-kilometer border between the two countries, even as conflicts frequently flare up. Iran is also home to around five million Afghan refugees who fled there to escape constant wars ravaging their homeland since 1979.[1] The most recent turn in this decades-long war was the conquest of Kabul in 2021 by the Taliban. When the Taliban were last in power, from 1996 to 2001, their Islamic Emirate passed, and brutally enforced, measures included banning girls from school and men from playing soccer, smoking or shaving their beard. They surpassed even the Iranian regime in imposing draconian Islamism across the Afghan nation. Were it not for the Taliban's Sunni sectarianism and Pashtun chauvinism, the two regimes may well have been bedfellows. But an alliance was out of the question: in 1998, following their takeover of Mazar Sharif, the Talban attacked the Iranian embassy and killed eight Iranian diplomats.

The first Taliban regime was not to last. Its harbouring of Al-Qaeda leaders, responsible for the 9/11 attacks, crossed the line. A global coalition spearheaded by the United States invaded Afghanistan and overthrew the Taliban just months after the Twin Towers fell. The Islamic Republic and America joined forces: the regime in Kabul was now enemy number one for both of them.

But there was something ironic about the Tehran regime's campaign against the Taliban: its own throttling of the democratic movement in Iran bore a striking resemblance to the Afghan Sunni Islamists. Geopolitical machinations conducted from on high mattered little to the peoples of Iran and Afghanistan, who had had often found common cause in their shared opposition to fanatical religious rule. In 1999, as Iranian students staged an uprising for freedom, they chanted a slogan that's now widespread: 'From Kabul to Tehran, death to the Taliban!' With the Taliban overthrown in 2001, and a period of relative political freedom in Afghanistan, an emerging civil society showed solidarity with Iranians' pursuit of freedom. Elected to Afghanistan's National Assembly in 2005, the feminist representative Malalai Joya made it a central point of her politics to speak in support of the Iranian women and against the regime.

If ordinary Iranians and Afghans needed another cause to cement their solidarity, the Iranian regime gave them one by increasingly favouring the Taliban in mid-2010s, a change from its nominal support of the Islamic Republic of Afghanistan since its founding in 2004. As the Taliban's insurgency retook much of the country in the 2010s, Tehran started cutting deals with the Islamist group, as did the US during Donald Trump's administration. By 2020, Trump and the Taliban came to an agreement for the US forces to leave the country soon. In the same year, an Iranian MP outraged many Iranians by praising the Taliban as 'an authentic movement of the region,' calling for 'collaboration with them to establish stability in Afghan society'.[2]

In August 2021, as Kabul finally fell to the Taliban, many Iranians instantly felt at one with tens of thousands of Afghan men and women who rose in resistance. Iranians followed the events in Afghanistan closely; they shared news, videos and images of anti-Taliban demonstrations. This was more than a simple interest in current affairs. They were living vicariously through Afghans. With remarkable courage, hundreds of Afghan women staged demonstrations, brandishing the national tricolor flag of Afghanistan, as opposed to the white-only banner of the Taliban's re-established Islamic Emirate. Ahmad Masood, the young son of a major former leader, now found enthusiastic supporters amongst ordinary Iranians. His father, Ahmad Shah Masood, had worked closely with the Iranian regime against the Taliban, before his mysterious murder in September 2001, only two days before the 9/11 attacks. As the Taliban and Tehran became allies in practice, if not officially, Masood the son found his supporters in the ranks of the Iranian regime's opponents.

A year later, when Iranian women rose up following Mahsa's killing in September 2022, Afghan progressive movements were the vanguard in condemning the brutality of the regime in Tehran. On 20 September, just days after Amini's death, a group of Afghan women issued a brave statement.

'The suffering we have gone through is no different than that of Sepideh Rashnu and Mahsa Amini,' the statement read. 'With the slogan Women, Life, Freedom, and with the chant of Death to dictatorship, we cry out our common pain. The Taliban in Afghanistan and the dictatorship in Iran can't snuff out the voice of freedom-loving women.'[3]

Wajihe Amiri, one of the many Afghan feminists who endorsed the statement, called Mahsa a 'symbol of courage, humanity and freedom against extremists'.[4] Around the world, Afghan and Iranian women joined one another in demonstrations. As the pain of oppression had spilled across borders, so too did the struggle for real liberty.

The slogan 'Women, Life, Freedom' did not originate in Iran, nor would it stop at its national boundaries. As women of Afghanistan resisted the Taliban's assault on their rights, they put the chant to use. On 30 October, female students were physically barred by a Taliban guard from entering Badakhshan University in the northeast.[5] As they banged on the gates and protested, they chanted a familiar slogan: 'Women, Life, Freedom.'

* * *

But whatever affinity there was between the progressive movements of the two countries, millions of Afghan refugees in Iran saw little solidarity in their daily lives. Governments came and went, movements surged and ebbed, but these migrants experienced an unbroken thread of racism, marginalisation and deprivation. Alongside the suffocating laws imposed by the Islamic Republic upon everyone, refugees remain subject to a host of targeted restrictions on their places of residence and work. On top of this, they faced the hostility of many Iranians. In 2019, a poll showed that 43% of people in Tehran demanded a ban on Afghans staying in the city and 40% favoured expulsion of all Afghan migrants from Iran; 44% favoured segregation of Afghans from other citizens in Tehran while 40% believed Afghans should study in their own separate schools. Only a narrow majority of 52% stood against school segregation.[6]

The widespread support for these Jim Crow-style regulations is even more shocking as Afghans have been part of Iranian society for generations, from the very first waves of refugees after the Soviet invasion in 1979. Many have remained in Iran, put down roots and raised families. But, in a tale now depressingly familiar and mirrored in countries like Turkey, Syria and Lebanon, even second and third-generation migrants are regarded as 'refugees' with almost no path to citizenship or even long-term residency permits. One of the few legal paths is for an Afghan woman to marry an Iranian man. Conversely, an Afghan man marrying an Iranian woman comes with no citizenship rights for the man and worse still, it deprives children of the couple the right to basic identity cards. Tens of thousands of such *sans-papiers* children live in Iran today. Like thousands of other Afghan children, they were barred from registration in schools as recently as 2015, when Khamenei finally lifted this ban. The Supreme Leader had not issued the order from a humanitarian impulse. The regime had recruited thousands of Afghan refugees, especially those from a Shia background, to serve as foot soldiers in the Syrian Civil War. Letting younger children go to school was intended as a token gesture of goodwill, after they dispatched the older children for slaughter.

Even for those with papers, things could change overnight. For years, Afghans have reported being randomly taken off a bus, their ID cards confiscated and consequently becoming subject to deportation. For a Human Rights Watch report in 2013, Najib T, a fifty-five-year-old Afghan in Iran, told his story. Where he had lived for years was one day arbitrarily declared as forbidden to foreigners. He was asked to leave the country.[7]

A worse fate awaited those who ran foul of the law for petty 'crimes'. This is what happened to Hosseina. She was arrested in the holy city of Qom for wearing pink sneakers. Her father, her sister Zohreh and Zohreh's fiancé went to the police station to plead for her release. But when the authorities found out they were Afghan, all four of them were summarily deported to Afghanistan. Meanwhile, Hosseina's mother and her three younger siblings were left back in Iran. The family was shattered.

Afghans who escaped arbitrary deportation still couldn't live a normal life. Even though they faced no linguistic barrier, Afghans with advanced degrees and professional experience could rarely find adequate employment. Afghan men were often forced to take menial jobs while Afghan women were seen as ripe targets for sexual exploitation. Take Homa who fled to Iran in 2021 following the fall of Kabul. She held a degree in diplomacy and had worked on prevention of violence against women for Balkh province's police in Afghanistan. In 2021, as the Taliban started persecuting officials of the former government, she fled to Iran. But her attempts at finding a job were repeatedly stymied. Any time she answered a job advert, she was asked for sexual favours. An employer once outright told her that she'd be hired 'if I would have sex with him once a week'.[8] She lost all hope in getting a job that fit her qualifications. She settled on a low-paid job in caring, often the only sort of job available to Afghans. Sepideh, a PhD student of sociology in one of Tehran's universities, had similar experiences. In the last stage of a recruitment process, she started getting strange questions about her marital status and availability to work in the evening. It soon became clear that her future boss was demanding sexual favours. When she refused, the prospective employer bluntly stated 'we don't give jobs to Afghans here'.

If you were lucky enough to find a job, you might still not be able to access your wages. In 2018, London-based outlet IranWire reported on the closure of bank accounts of Afghans by Iranian state banks. Dumbfounded when he found his debit card was not working, Reza was told by Bank Melli that his account had been blocked as a measure against all Afghans with temporary residency cards. He wasn't even allowed to access his balance. In 2023, Parisa (not her real name) told *Independent Persian* that, since her arrival in Mashhad the year before, she couldn't open a bank account for months. Her relatives in the United States had wanted to transfer money to her – they couldn't.

The struggle to survive without reliable access to banking and employment was compounded by dozens of humiliations in daily life. Without proper identity cards, Afghans often couldn't get tickets for the Tehran metro. Afghans who offered Iranians cash to buy a ticket for them were frequently met with cold shoulders or even outright insults. In the northeastern city of Mashhad, a hub for the Afghan diaspora, Afghans generally can't get the city's Man Card, an all-purpose facility for metro, buses and mobile top-ups. In Mashhad, as in New York City, many shops refuse to accept cash. These include bakeries whose fresh bread is a basic staple in Iran. Denied bank cards, many Afghans can't get the *barbari* and *lavash* that others buy every morning.

The Covid-19 pandemic revealed the full scale of discrimination against Afghan migrants. Afghans who contracted the virus were on occasion turned away from hospital or charged exorbitant amounts. An Afghan in Kashan died after being denied hospitalisation. Many clinics which distributed free masks to Iranians refused to provide any to those without national IDs, i.e. Afghans and other refugees. Fatemeh, an Afghan migrant in Shahriyar, reported that she wasn't even able to buy a mask despite having a proper residency card. All she received were insults instead.[9]

Something as simple as going to a park could become an ordeal for Afghans. In 2019, University of Tehran sociologist Arash Nasr Esfahani published a study throwing a spotlight on these experiences.[10] Narges, an interviewee, described being mocked in parks so much that she now avoids them altogether. On social media, videos and tweets by Afghans who recounted everyday racist encounters around Iran went viral. 'Wherever we go, Iranians claims that Afghans have occupied their country,' one woman Nazanin reported. Painfully, some of the worst discrimination was reserved for Hazaras, a Shia ethnic minority in Afghanistan who are among the most visibly Afghan. A Shia minority in Sunni-majority Afghanistan, Hazaras have a long history of being persecuted by Kabul. The Taliban regime brought its own brutal forms of persecution, driving many to flee to Shia-majority Iran. Yet instead of finding religious fraternity, they faced abuse and exclusion. A Hazara high school student spoke of how other kids mocked her as 'slanted eye', a facial feature typical of Hazaras.

Schools could be filled with similar experiences for Afghan children in Iran. In 2015, an eleven-year-old Afghan boy topped the Qur'an recital competition in his school and was slated to be sent to the city-wide competition. But the teacher decided that an Afghan couldn't represent the school and he was excluded from the contest. A few years before, in a school in southern Tehran, a principal attempted to 'praise' an Afghan student who had used an innovative way of pasting papers onto his textbook, instead of writing on its pages, so that it could be passed down to someone else next year. What came out was him berating the other students: 'Shame on you! How can an Afghan kid be smarter than you?'[11]

Televised portrayals of Afghans didn't help. Hackneyed stereotypes dominated airtime. In these TV shows, Afghans caused Iranian unemployment, perpetrated violent crimes and transmitted diseases.

* * *

As the new revolutionary movement broke out in September 2022, Afghans had many reasons to stay out of it. Political turbulence meant economic uncertainty and some Afghan construction workers reported losing their jobs in the first week of protests. And did it make sense for them to join an uprising when they'd experienced so much abuse at the hands of Iranian people? Worried about the diplomatic implications of Afghans joining an Iranian uprising, the Taliban immigration minister called on Iran-based Afghans to stay home and avoid the demonstrations.

But Afghans had lived with Iranians for years. They had suffered under the same state, experienced the same repression, endured the same police brutality. In the Islamic Republic, they found a foe so similar to the hated Taliban. How could they *not* join the cry of Women, Life, Freedom?

And so many did just that. Dozens of Afghans were arrested in cities such as Tehran and Mashhad for taking part in the demonstrations. Improbable as it might have seemed initially, the movement soon found its own Afghan martyrs. In September alone, two Afghan teenagers were among the earliest killed in the uprising: Mohammadreza Sarvari, fourteen, was killed by a bullet in Shahr-e Rey on 21 September. A day later, Setareh Tajik, seventeen, was beaten to death by the regime's batons in Tehran.

We know little of their lives, but their faces became symbols of the revolution. In a country that had never treated them as their own, they had given their lives for freedom. A photograph of Setareh showed her with bright eyes, sporting a joyful smile and flashing a V sign. It seemed to represent everything Iranians were fighting for. Her name plastered walls as graffiti and she was mourned far and wide. The tragic irony in her martyrdom was obvious: Setareh had fled from the Taliban, only to be killed by its ideological kin in Iran. Her name means 'star' in Persian and many used Persian poetic traditions to remember her as a bright star now snuffed out by the regime. 'Stars of the sky of freedom have built a galaxy,' a social media user wrote.[12] Others recited a line by the veteran communist poet Siavash Kasraee: 'Every night they bring down a star / But this forlorn sky is still filled with stars.'

Fereshteh Hosseini, an Afghan-Iranian actress and the spouse of the legendary actor Navid Mohammadzade, paid a stirring tribute. Like Setareh, Fereshteh was an Afghan: she had been born to Afghan parents in Tehran. Defying the odds, Fereshteh rose to become a film star in Iran and was a celebrity in her own right. Just a few months before, she had been walking on the red carpet of the Cannes Film Festival alongside Navid, representing the Iranian film *Leila's Brothers.*[*] They made the news when Navid sweetly kissed Fereshteh in front of the eager cameras of the press. But all their fame and artistic success did not spare the happy couple from an avalanche of racist abuse. Fereshteh was derided as an opportunist in pursuit of an Iranian passport and Navid was chastised for not marrying an Iranian. As a second-generation Afghan migrant, Fereshteh felt a particular sympathy with Setareh's story. In an Instagram post, she shared her picture and commemorated her as kin: 'The generation born in Iran, our generation, my generation, the generation that seemingly doesn't

---

* Just as I was making the final edits to this book, in August 2023, the film's director Sayeed Rostaee was sentenced to six months in prison. He was convicted of having shown *Leila's Brothers* in Cannes without an official permission.

have the right to protest! Not there, not here. And we die, both there and here.'

As Iranians marched on the streets for freedom, there was hope that Afghans might be met as comrades in the struggle, not as unwelcome foreigners. Shervin Hajipour's hit anthem for the movement, 'For the Sake of', poignantly declared it to be 'for the sake of Afghan children'.

On 18 October 2022, when Sahra Rezaee, an Afghan student of journalism at Tehran's Alame Tabatabaei University, went missing, her fellow students, Iranian opposition activists and media outlets worked hard on her behalf. 'Where is Sahra' trended after campaigns by both Iranian and Afghan activists. She was finally released in December.[13]

Some Afghans went further by explicitly calling on their compatriots to join the movement in Iran. In a Facebook post, Afghan artist Ali Hezare issued a call of hope: 'My compatriots in Iran: if Iran changes, it will also change for you. You will no longer be bound by an autocratic government that regards you as material for slaughter in its wars.'

As the regime arrested anybody who was anybody in Iran's civil society, a newly alert nation came to pay more attention to the work of progressive activists – including those who had long swam against the current by advocating for Afghan rights. On 3 October, Sepideh Salarvand was arrested in Tehran after her family home was raided by the authorities.[14] An anthropologist and a documentary filmmaker, the thirty-one-year-old Salarvand had dedicated her young career to exposing the grim conditions of Afghan children working in Iran. For years, alongside her comrade-cum-husband Aydin Halalzadeh, she had taught these children in a garbage dump outside Tehran as a volunteer. Conducting participant observation and ethnography in the same landfill, she wrote her MA dissertation on the topic at Tehran's University of Science and Culture. Red Wisdom, a Tehran-based publishing house, turned the thesis into a riveting book, *As If I Had Become Mute*. Every bit of an *intellectuelle engagée*, Salarvand combined her scholarship and filmmaking with advocacy for Afghan children. Her arrest put her work in the spotlight. In the cells of Evin and other prisons, the movement was finding its people, giving rise to the hope that maybe its emancipatory agenda could come to include millions of Afghans in Iran.

* * *

In March 2023, as the spring came, Iranians and Afghans should have been celebrating Nowruz, a festival welcoming in the new year. But in the ancient traditions, Nowruz is a time bereft when one has lost a beloved in the preceding year. How could they now be celebrating when hundreds of their compatriots had been killed in their quest for freedom?

A popular Nowruz tradition is setting up a table called Haft Sin, consisting of seven items that start with the letter Sin (which sounds like S) in Persian. A classic Haft Sin consists of wheat sprouts (*sabzi*), apples (*seeb*), garlic (*seer*), coins (*sekkeh*), vinegar (*serkeh*), sumac (*Somaq*) and hyacinths (*sonbol.*) This year, many Iranians added new items: pictures of martyrs of the movement whose name started with S. Video of a Haft-Sin shared on social media included a name that many had now came to learn by heart: *Setareh* Tajik.[15] An Afghan was now mourned by Iranians across the country.

But at the very same time, the ugly side of Iranian society made itself known. During the Nowruz holidays, many denizens of the bustling and polluted Tehran headed to the artificial Chitgar Lake in the western outskirts of the city to get some fresh air and enjoy the delights of Bamland Mall, a sprawling shopping centre. Hundreds of Afghan workers had the same idea; they used the rare occasion of annual holidays to take their families out to the lake. Bamland seemed like an idyll away from the turbulent months since September 2022. Children could play by the lake as flocks of birds flew overhead. Others engaged in the favourite Nowruz pastime of shopping and dining out in big family groups. There was live music in every corner as well as seasonal displays and performances.

But once more, Afghans were not welcome. As an investigation by Tehran daily *Shargh* revealed later, Afghans were thrown out and explicitly told to stay away during the four-day holiday period between 21 and 24 March. According to *Shargh*, a Bamland official stated the policy openly: 'For the comfort of Iranian citizens, Afghans have been barred from Bamland for four days.'[16]

In an Orwellian public statement, Bamland at once denied and defended the exclusionary policy. After claiming that it had no authority to bar people, it went on to justify the ban that, it alleged, had been enforced by municipal authorities.

'Can you imagine that, suddenly, as businesses, construction projects and the like close down [for national holidays] thousands of Afghans, mostly young men, come to an urban and familial space?' the statement read. 'Naturally, such presence doesn't fit with the expectations of fellow Iranians who come to the lake for leisure or sports. So, to create balance and provide an opportunity for all groups to use this public space, municipal authorities had to take adequate measures and provide for equal conditions for our fellow Iranians.'[17]

This time, as Iranian journalists broke the story, many Iranians loudly protested Bamland's policy, sharing *Shargh*'s condemnation of the unabashed racism. Bamland's Instagram page became a battleground between those objecting to the mall's racism and those defending the ban.

'I don't think not letting the dear Afghans in for four days can be called racism,' wrote Setareh Zahedian. 'Thank you Bamland,' wrote Hanie, a gynaecologist, 'at least you are thinking of us. Wherever one goes, there are droves of Afghanis, single and without documents. All they do is harass us.'

Yet these did not outweigh the swell of outrage against Bamland. Mehrnoosh Nasiri, a fashion stylist from Tehran, apologised to Afghans on behalf of Iranians and asked Bamland to issue its own apology. Her comment received more likes than any other. The second most popular comment came from Mohammadreza Mohsenirad, a psychologist who called out

Bamland for 'racist behaviour' and declared that he would never set foot there until they apologised. Many Iranians, online and offline, reacted in the same spirit. The Afghans of Iran didn't put up with this discrimination quietly. After the news of the ban went viral, an Afghan man and woman performed a duet near Bamland and broadcast it online.

The young woman performed without her Hijab – the struggle for women's freedom and for refugees' rights were inextricably interlinked.

'As you know yourself, the very fact that I am singing here is a crime,' she said in a full Tehrani accent, revealing she had grown up in the city. 'I don't have a scarf on and that's another crime. I hope you'll like the song I am about to sing. Let me tell you the reason I came here: I am originally from Afghanistan and recently we had a big problem: I heard that Afghans had been banned from Bamland.'[18]

'I am human, just like you,' she added. 'And this is my human right. I was born here and grew up here. Now I can't even go to Bamland to buy anything or eat anything? I hope that you support us. Don't just pass by.'

Those watching took heed. They cheered and applauded the duo for standing up for Afghan rights. Iranians shared the video online. As Afghans join the ongoing movement, it's becoming clearer by the day: Women, Life, Freedom needs to be Women, Life, Freedom *for all*. Only then can Iran win a better future.

Eight

I Give My Life for Iran: The Fight for Peace

Elderly pensioners might not be whom you picture as revolutionary firebrands. But in Iran, retirees are regularly on the streets, protesting against skyrocketing inflation eroding their standard of living. On 26 February 2023, these men and women joined a nationwide wave of strikes and added their own placards to the mix. The rallies chanted 'Retiree, speak up and shout out your demands' alongside slogans linked to current pay and conditions. But their demands weren't purely economic. They called out: 'Leave Syria alone and think of us!'[1]

This slogan dates back as far as 2017, when pensioners in Isfahan first deployed it.[2] But since the uprising in 2022, it's now everywhere, echoing on the streets and written on the walls across Iran. Iranians linked their ongoing impoverishment to the astronomical cost of Iran's military intervention in Syria, which came in at the hefty sum of up to thirty billion dollars, while making Iran even more of a pariah in the international community. More than two thousand Iranian soldiers had been killed on the Syrian battlefield, defending the authoritarian regime of President Bashar al-Assad. Workers posed a simple question: how come the Islamic Republic couldn't provide for its citizens while it could spill blood and empty its coffers to prop up a regime in Syria?

The Iranian regime's firm commitment to Assad has often been misunderstood by blinkered Western commentators to be a matter of Shias backing Shias against Sunnis. How else to make sense of Iran's growing role in Syria and other Arab countries such as Iraq, Lebanon and Yemen? Others trotted out another lazy claim ad nauseam: Iranians stood behind their government's foreign policy and wholeheartedly approved of Iranian expansionism. Relying on these platitudes, Western observers overlooked how much shrewd geopolitics, not religious conviction, motivated Iran's leaders over the decades. But more significantly, few in the West grasped just how disillusioned Iranians were with a government indulging in military adventures abroad while they starved.

* * *

This disillusionment came to the fore in 2009, in the throes of the largest protest wave in the history of the Republic. After the incumbent president, Mahmoud Ahmadinejad, was declared the winner, supporters of the pro-reform candidate, Mirhossein Mousavi, staged a series of mass demonstrations. Mousavi claimed that the polls had been rigged. It was a watershed moment in the history of the Islamic Republic. Like previous elections under the regime, the 2009 polls were anything but free and fair. Only regime insiders were allowed to run. Mousavi certainly counted as one. He had been a favourite of Ayatollah Khomeini and served as prime minister from 1981 to 1989. By denying Mousavi the presidency, Khamenei had broken an unspoken convention – he had rigged the vote for his preferred candidate in a heavily vetted choice on the ballot.

But Khamenei's obduracy didn't deter Mousavi from standing his ground. Despite the beatings, arrests and even killings faced by his supporters, the demonstrations continued and so the Green Movement was born, christened for Mousavi's campaigning colours.

To circumvent the ban on street protests, the Green Movement adopted a Trojan horse tactic. Mousavi and his supporters would show up to annual mass rallies organised by the regime to commemorate historical milestones and chant their own slogans. This was not simply a clever manoeuvre, it represented the movement's raison d'être. As the Islamic Republic entered its fourth decade, the Green Movement sought to wrest control of its past and seize its future. Having been largely absent from public view since his resignation as prime minister in 1989, Mousavi embodied the forgotten ideals of the revolutionary generation. As head of the government during the long years of the war with Iraq, he reminded many of the patriotic devotion and left-leaning economic policies of the 1980s. He cultivated this impression by shouting over Ahmadinejad in a televised debate: 'I speak here as a revolutionary.'³ Now, as each regime rally celebrated the revolution's heroic days, the Green Movement's attendance allowed them to claim a space on the public stage and contest the future of the republic with a different vision.

At the end of Ramadan that year, the regime prepared to celebrate Jerusalem (Quds) Day on 18 September, an occasion for anti-Israel demonstrations. Khomeini had inaugurated this 'tradition' in 1979, seeking to turn Eid al-Fitr into a global anti-Israel rally. If Muslims of the world overcame their sectarian differences, Khomeini declared, they could 'wipe Israel off the scene of time'. In its more graphic version, Khomeini exhorted that 'if every Muslim threw a bucket of water at Israel, it would be drowned.'⁴ But Palestinians and other Arabs had never really taken to Quds Day and it remained a mostly Iranian affair.

As the Quds Day of 2009 approached, the regime's authorities warned the Green Movement against using its Trojan tactics. For years, the day's main speech in Tehran had been given by former president Ayatollah Akbar Hashemi Rafsanjani. But since he was known as a Green Movement sympathiser, the Ayatollah was replaced by a junior hardliner cleric. Ahmadinejad would also deliver a keynote speech. On 13 September, the daily *Kayhan*, a mouthpiece for Khamenei, cautioned protesters against display-ing green colours, or using anti-regime chants. 'All those who use divisive slogans and symbols, whether they know it or not, whether they want it or not, are mercenaries of Israel,' wrote the paper's influential editor-in-chief, Hossein Shariatmadari. 'They will have a share in the savage crimes of Israel.'[5] On 17 September, one day before the rally, the IRGC issued a statement and specifi-cally warned Mousavi's supporters against 'using deviatory slogans, preferred by Americans and Zionists.'[6]

But threats couldn't subdue a movement that had already mourned many martyrs. On 18 September, hundreds of thou-sands of Green Movement supporters joined demonstrations in Tehran, Shiraz, Isfahan, Tabriz, Qom, Ahvaz, Mashhad, Rasht and Kermanshah. In a speech in Tehran's Imam Sadiq University, an IRGC leader claimed that two million Green Movement support-ers had infiltrated the Quds Day rallies. Mousavi himself was sighted in Tehran. Meanwhile, in the official rally, Ahmadinejad used his speech to return one of his favourite themes: denial of the Holocaust.[7] 'They set up the myth of the Holocaust. They lie and they play games,' he said. 'They claim to support Jews, but they sacrifice all human values for the Zionist regime.'

Mousavi had previously criticised Ahmadinejad's persistent Holocaust denial as costly to the country. But he had never wavered from his own pro-Palestinian stance. In fact, he had also reproached Ahmadinejad's vice president Esfandiar Rahim Mashaei for calling for 'friendship with the people of Israel' in summer 2008.

In participating in the Quds Day demonstrations, the movement proved its anti-Zionist credentials and its esteem for Khomeini as the progenitor of these mass rallies. But the day was also an opportune moment for the Green Movement to call out the regime's hypocrisy. How could the regime claim to stand for the oppressed in Palestine while it was oppressing its own people in Iran? Many of the slogans chanted on 18 September were along the same line. 'Why are you not moving, people! Iran has become Palestine,' one said. 'Palestine, Palestine, we are just like you,' another went.

But one slogan transgressed these limits. In a direct attack on Iran's support for Hezbollah and Hamas, protesters called out: 'Neither Gaza, nor Lebanon, I give my life for Iran.'

It attracted the ire of regime leaders who didn't see it as a criticism of particular foreign policy decisions but as a full-frontal assault on the very ideological foundations of the Islamic Republic. It became a focal point of the regime's reproval for years to come – Khamenei and other regime leaders frequently denigrated it. But the slogan did not initially enjoy unanimous support among the opposition to the regime. Its advocates justified it as civic patriotism and as a denunciation of the regime's foreign interventions, which were often unpopular with people in Arab countries too. But detractors argued it hardly spoke to a spirit of solidarity and reeked of Iranian nationalism's traditional anti-Arab attitudes.

Events would put both these notions to the test. An opportunity for solidarity between Iranians and Arabs was just around the corner.

The Green Movement's mammoth street presence peaked on 27 December 2009, when the supporters joined the annual processions of Ashura, commemorating the unjust killing of Imam Hussein in the Battle of Karbala in the year 680, an icon of the struggle against oppression in Shia culture. On that heady day, the Islamic Republic killed at least thirty-seven people of the tens of thousands who joined Green Movement contingents all over the country. It became obvious that without a strategy to seize power, the Green Movement was unable to march forward. The movement's last big push was its attempt to infiltrate the anniversary of revolution celebrations in February 2010. Dozens were arrested in Tehran, Isfahan, Mashhad, Shiraz and Ahvaz but it was clear that the movement couldn't bring out the same numbers anymore. By late 2010, even the most enthusiastic supporter of the Green Movement knew that immediate change wasn't on the horizon.

But just when prospects for a new revolution in Iran dimmed, in the Arab world a flame was lit. On 17 December 2010, a street vendor set himself on fire in Sidi Bouzid, Tunisia, to protest against the degrading harassment he faced by municipal officials. His death in hospital on 4 January 2010 sparked a revolution in Tunisia that soon spread to most other Arab countries. Merely ten days later, on 14 January, Tunisia's President Zine El Abidine Ben Ali fled to Saudi Arabia with his wife, Leila. For the first time in modern history, Arab masses had overthrown a president by popular protest. But more was to come. In neighbouring Egypt, President Hosni Mubarak resigned on 11 February. In a matter of months, the presidents of Libya and Yemen were also overthrown while Syria's President Assad looked like he was on the ropes as hundreds of thousands turned out in demonstrations week after week. We now know this as the Arab Spring.

For Iranians, this was a new jolt of life. In Tehran, a new chant resounded down the streets: 'Mubarak, Ben Ali, it's time for Seyyed Ali [Khamenei].'[8] Seeing the fall of Arab leaders such as Mubarak and Libya's Muammar Qaddafi gave heart to Iranians who felt united with the Arab world in their fight for freedom and dignity.

On 25 January, just as Egyptians launched the now legendary assembly in Cairo's Tahrir Square, Mousavi issued a statement praising the movement. 'The pharaohs usually hear the voice of the nation when it's too late,' he said, comparing the street demonstrations in Cairo, Tunis and Sanaa with those of Tehran in 2009. He wished for victory in the Arab peoples' 'rightful struggles'.[9]

What could be more exhilarating than the prospect of an arc of pro-democracy forces binding together Arab nations and Iran? In hindsight, this was obviously too good to be true. The Spring was followed by a long and harsh winter lasting to this day. The Egyptian military and Muslim Brotherhood stepped into the post-Mubarak vacuum and battled one another. In 2013, a coup by army chief Abdelfattah al-Sissi led to a military dictatorship, resembling the pre-2011 regime. He remains in office at the time of writing. In Libya and Yemen, the overthrow of dictators presaged civil wars that ravaged them for years. For a while the tiny state of Tunisia remained the one bright spot on the map, whose one-party regime had been replaced with an actual democracy. But the failure of Tunisia's political parties to resolve people's social demands led to the election of maverick President Kais Saied in 2019. He went on to shut down Tunisia's parliament and extinguish all its democratic institutions.

For its part, before the bitter truth was evident, the Green Movement attempted to use the new revolutionary atmosphere in the region for a new set of street campaigns. On 5 February 2011, Mousavi wrote to the Ministry of Interior to ask for a permit for a rally in Tehran in solidarity with the Egyptian and Tunisian revolutions. Not only was no such permit given, more people were arrested in anticipation of a possible illegal rally. Soon after, Mousavi was put under house arrest, where he remains at the time of writing, more than twelve years later. The same conditions were imposed on his wife and fellow activist, Zahra Rahnavard, as well as Mehdi Karroubi, his fellow pro-reform presidential candidate in 2009, and his wife, Fateme. Green Movement leaders had evaded arrests in over a year of dramatic demonstrations. But expressing solidarity with the Arab Spring counted as the final straw.

While democracy remained an elusive dream, authoritarian regimes in the region all attempted to use the shifting sands of Arab politics to their own benefit. For the Iranian regime, this meant resolutely backing its main allies, first and foremost the Assad regime of Syria. As Assad killed hundreds of thousands of his own people, the Iranian regime put its resources at his disposal. Khamenei decided early on that the overthrow of Assad would be a lethal blow he couldn't tolerate. He had to be preserved at all costs. Qassem Soleimani, chief of IRGC's external operations, became a regular in Damascus as he coordinated the dispatching of tens of thousands of Iranian, Afghan, Pakistani, Iraqi and Lebanese forces to Syria.[10]

At the outset of the Arab Spring, Syria had been a major hope for democratic transformation. With the intervention of the Iranian regime and other regional powers, it soon became a quagmire, divided into several chunks, moving between the Assad regime, various local militias and their foreign backers. In 2014 the Islamic State of Iraq and Syria (ISIS), a now notorious Salafi jihadist terrorist organisation, took over large portions of eastern Syria as well as western Iraq, declaring a transnational Islamic caliphate. A year later, Vladimir Putin's Russia joined the fray and launched air raids to support Assad. Putin was convinced to intervene in the war through a private audience with Soleimani in Moscow. Once, in the initial fervour of the 1979 Revolution, the Islamic Republic draped itself in an anti-imperialist mantle. Now it extended an invitation to new imperial powers.

* * *

But Iranians didn't accept their country's adventurism quietly, and discontent only grew as the situation in Iran worsened.

In 2016, Mehdi Khazali, son of a leading cleric and a well-known political commentator in his own right, attacked the

Iranian policy on Syria. Tehran should have let Assad fall so that Iran could have better relations with a democratic Syria, Khazali said, before adding that Soleimani's own behaviour was responsible for the rise of ISIS. Khazali went on to predict that Soleimani and IRGC would soon be widely hated in Syria and Lebanon.[11] It was a prophetic statement. In 2019, protesters in Iraq and Lebanon revolted against the influence of Soleimani and the regime in Tehran. When Soleimani was killed in January 2020, Syrians celebrated his death.

From his house arrest, Mousavi joined the chorus of criticism. In 2022, when an Arabic translation of Green Movement statements was published, he wrote a foreword in which he once more paid tribute to the ideals of the Arab Spring. He reproached the Iranian regime for betraying the wave of Arab revolutions and condemned its interventions in Syria as 'shedding blood in faraway lands aimed at strengthening the foundations of a child-killing regime'.[12]

The controversial slogan of September 2009 ('Neither Gaza, nor Lebanon, I give my life for Iran') proved tenacious in the years to come. Shouted on the streets and written on placards, it has reverberated all over the country and gained household fame. In anti-regime protests since 2017, it's a staple of the repertoire. A long list of regime leaders, topped by Khamenei, have attacked the slogans while a growing number of Iranians have come to its defence.[13] Now many Iranians demand a foreign policy that is conciliatory rather than belligerent: an Iran that doesn't support armed militias in neighbouring countries and pursues peaceful relations with other states, including the United States and Israel.

In other words, as the Iranian regime regularly promises to flatten Tel Aviv and Haifa with its missiles, an increasing number of Iranians have called for an end to the dangerous tensions between the two countries. In 2012, as the threat of an attack by Israel over Iran's growing nuclear programme cast a shadow over the region, thousands of ordinary citizens of Iran and Israel took to Facebook with a simple message, repeated in Persian, Arabic, Hebrew, English and other languages: 'We Don't Want War.' It had started with an online campaign, named 'Israel Loves Iran', by young Israelis critical of sabre-rattling of their own Prime Minister Benjamin Netanyahu.[14] It quickly found an echo among young Iranians, equally terrified at the prospect of a war.

It would have been easy to dismiss this as youthful idealism. But prominent Iranians also came to openly support a policy of peace. Mostafa Tajzadeh, a leading reformist politician and former deputy interior minister, criticised the regime's policy of not letting Iranian athletes compete with their Israeli counterparts.[15] During a Friday prayer sermon in January 2023, Maulavi Abdulhamid called for a two-state solution to the Israel–Palestine conflict. 'Palestinians must get to have their own sovereign government,' he said. 'There should be two independent governments: both Palestine and Israel.'[16] This was a departure from his own long track record of anti-Israeli statements.

Ever since 2020, when the Abraham Accords led to normalisation of ties between Israel and four new Arab countries (United

Arab Emirates, Bahrain, Morocco and Sudan), a growing number of Iranians had asked for de-escalation with Israel. Faeze Hashemi called on the regime to adopt a pragmatic and realistic approach to Israel in the wake of accords.

'Yes, the Zionist regime has occupied the Palestinian lands,' she said, speaking to the newspaper *Arman-e Melli* in October 2020. 'But, since 1948, the United Nations has recognised this regime as a country. Both Arabs and Jews live there... we have to be up-to-date on the global scene and take decisions in line with our interests.'[17]

Two years later, she spoke more brazenly in a public chat with Zibakalam. 'Our enmity with Israel doesn't make any sense,' she said. 'Why do I say this? Because our actions are now worse than Israel's.' If Iran was opposed to occupation, how come it was aiding Russia's occupation of Ukraine, she asked. And if it was opposed to Israel killing Palestinians, how come it had supported Assad's brutal killing of his own people in Syria?[18]

Hashemi's interlocutor in the discussion couldn't have agreed with her more. In fact, if peace had one intellectual poster boy, it was Zibakalam who had stuck his neck out for years. Like many of his fellow reformists, he had started out as a stalwart supporter of the Islamic Republic. In the lead-up to the 1979 revolution, Zibakalam had spent two years in the dungeons of the Shah for his anti-regime activities. As the nascent republic tried to negotiate with opposition Kurdish groups, Zibakalam was a young member of the government's delegation in the talks. But he had spent much of the eighties in Britain, where he received his PhD in peace studies from the University of Bradford.[19] In the years to come, he had come to support liberalisation and a pro-peace foreign policy.

Well-suited for the age of visual media, Zibakalam had a flair for theatrics and went viral often. In 2016, he was invited to a debate in a university in Mashhad. As with some other government buildings, the floor at the university was adorned with the flags of Israel and United States, inviting visitors to walk over them. As cameras surrounded him, Zibakalam refused to walk over the flags, elevating himself by holding on to the sidebars to avoid even stepping on them.[20] When he was attacked by the pro-regime media, he doubled down and defended his move: 'To trample upon and to burn the flag of any country is wrong.'

This was par for course for Zibakalam. Two years earlier, in a debate hosted by Tehran's Imam Sadeq University, Zibakalam had stunned the audience by attacking the regime's anti-Israel policy head-on.

'We believe we must destroy Israel and we have thus made it into an ideological question and do so much for it,' Zibakalam said. 'But I have a question: who gave us this task? Why should our foreign policy be based on it? If we don't support Hezbollah, how long will it last?'

He ended boldly: 'I recognise Israel because the United Nations recognises it.'[21]

Just a few months later, he publicly reaffirmed the notorious 2009 slogan: 'Neither Gaza, nor Lebanon, I give my life for Iran.'[22]

'As an Iranian Muslim, I don't know why I should apologise for this slogan,' he said in an interview with *Afkar News*. 'I still believe that Iran comes first, second, third and last. Just like Palestine comes first, second and third for Palestinians.'[23] He reminded his detractors that the slogan was born after Hezbollah's leader, Hassan Nasrallah, had supported Ahmadinejad just as Iran was engulfed in protests against him. In 2021, Zibakalam published a lengthy book on the history of Jewish people, from 2000 BCE to 1948.[24] Entitled *Birth of Israel: History of Four Thousand Years of Judaism*, the book was predictably banned in Iran but was widely disseminated in bootleg copies and an audiobook version, read out by Zibakalam himself.[25] He continued teaching it in his own classes at the University of Tehran, stressing that it was important for Iranians to know why and how Israel had come to be. The book had been dedicated to Nelson Mandela as someone who had 'forgiven all his enemies'. It was an astonishing departure from the antisemitic material published by the state media.

Zibakalam's advocacy of recognition of Israel didn't mean he was blind to Palestinian rights. Like many others, he seemed to long for a return to Iran's foreign policy during the 1970s when Tehran had kept close ties with both Israel and the Arab world, while vociferously criticising Israel's occupation of Palestinian territories. In 2023, when the Shah's son, Reza Pahlavi, visited Israel for a much-publicised week-long trip, Zibakalam took him to task for not showing any sympathy to Palestinians or meeting any of their leaders. While having no issue with Pahlavi setting foot in Israel, Zibakalam chastised him for his 'unbelievable silence on Palestinians during this trip' which he called 'sad and unacceptable'.[26]

'In all your speeches and interviews, you didn't raise Palestinian rights even once,' Zibakalam said. 'To respect your Jewish compatriots, you paid a pilgrimage to the Western Wall. But shouldn't you have also shown respect to your Christian and Muslim compatriots by visiting the Church of Nativity and Masjid al-Aqsa? I have to add that I am saying this as someone who refused to walk over the Israeli flag, as someone who was fired from the university because he advocated recognition of Israel.'

Zibakalam had also proven his consistency by his vociferous support of Ukraine as it came under attack from Russia. Already during the 2014 Maidan revolution, he had written an open letter to Kyiv's ambassador to Tehran, to apologise for the pro-Kremlin voices aired on the state media.

'Don't be upset by the unfair and unjust views of the Iranian authorities and statesmen,' Zibakalam said in the letter which was proudly published on the website of the Ukrainian embassy in Tehran. 'You should know that just like the freedom-loving people of Russia came out onto the streets of Moscow to condemn the aggressive policies of their country in Ukraine, the hearts of many freedom-loving and righteous people of Iran are also with the people of Ukraine.'[27]

As Russian tanks rolled into Ukraine in early 2022, most countries censured this naked aggression. Iran, however, was one of only five countries, alongside Syria, Belarus, North Korea and Eritrea, to vote against a United Nations resolution that condemned the invasion. President Raisi was quick to get on the phone with Putin and blame the conflict on NATO. Iran happily supplied drones to Russia, furnishing it for the long war to come.[28] More predictably the regime media attacked Ukraine's President Volodymyr Zelenskyy in nasty antisemitic rants. While the Ukrainian president was being admired by many Iranians for standing up for his nation, the regime's Fars News Agency called him 'a Jewish follower of the hedonistic school… influenced by rich Jews such as Jeffrey Epstein and George Soros'.[29]

But among ordinary people, you didn't need to look hard to see the opposition of many Iranians to Russia's wanton aggression. Mohammad Mohajeri, a journalist, condemned the invasion and tweeted: 'I wish my country had a foreign minister brave enough to condemn Russia's military aggression against another country'.[30] Azar Mansoori, a reformist activist, criticised the state media for its coverage of the war and said: 'Go compare it to your coverage of the occupation of Afghanistan and Iraq by the US. An aggressor is an aggressor and must be condemned. There is no such a thing as a good violator'.[31] Tajzade immediately called Russia an aggressor. Hoda Mahmoodi, a student activist, said: 'Shall we learn a lesson and not trust Russia.' Even Ali Motahhari, a conservative MP, complained that Iran's state broadcaster was covering the war as if Ukraine was 'a colony of Russia' and criticised Iran for 'helping the violation of Ukraine by Russia'.[32]

But protests weren't limited to social media. On 26 February 2022, a number of Iranians gathered in front of the Ukrainian embassy in Tehran, holding up handmade blue-and-yellow flags of the country to protest. They chanted: 'Down with Putin', 'Love, live, peace' and, most bitingly, 'the Russian embassy is a den of espionage', using a common slur directed against the US embassy when it was occupied by protesters in 1979. Security forces quickly attacked the crowds. Videos showed a young woman, brandishing an Ukrainian flag, shouting at the security forces: 'We hate you.'[33]

Among those who made it to the demonstration was Vahid Heroabadi, a perennially smiling cleric, known for his scathing social criticism online. Condemning 'Putin's brutal invasion,' he had called on people to join the action. Following the demonstration, he was threatened with phone calls from security bodies. A few months later, he was sentenced to two years in prison and a ban from wearing his clerical garb. According to his wife, Vahid's position against Putin had been cited as the primary evidence against him.[34]

But if intellectuals and demonstrators weren't enough, this time around even the diplomatic establishment of the Islamic Republic was fed up. Veteran diplomats criticised Iran's brazen pro-Moscow position that seemed to throw all caution to the wind. In March 2023, Ali Majedi, Iran's former ambassador to Germany, warned, with only some exaggeration, that Iran was now paying a higher price for the war in Ukraine than Russia itself.[35] Mohammadreza Falahatpishe, a former head of the parliamentary national security and foreign policy committee, repeatedly rebuked Iran's policy on the war. In March 2022, he thundered: 'The Iranian state media's attempt to whitewash Russian crimes in Ukraine is shameful. Putin the Tsar is trampling upon the rights of human beings.' In June 2023, he lamented: 'Iran's national interest is being sacrificed for Russia.'[36]

The foreign policy consensus in Iran has shifted. Now Iranians demand an Iranian foreign policy that builds a country at peace with itself and with the world. Ready as they are to give their life for the country they love, Iranians are tired of funding wars while their own nation crumbles around them.

Nine

Sarina's Revolution:
The Fight for a Normal Life

'Over 500 people died in the 2022 Iran protests' is a shocking, true headline. But it is an alienating one – compressing many individuals into one sensational number. No one came out on the streets to die; no one dreamt of heroic martyrdom. All they wanted was a country where they could live freely. Many continue to chant 'Say their name'. But what lies behind the name, a photograph, the few sentences that make it into a clipped news report? Who are Iran's protesters really?

In the last week of September 2022, one death after another was confirmed on the news. Iranians hungered for more information about those who paid the ultimate price for voicing the demands of the nation. Who was Foad Qadimi, a father of two in Divandareh, Kurdistan, who was shot in the stomach on 21 September and died two days later in Sanandaj? The reports told us he owned a laundry and people from his town remembered him as witty.[1]

Who was Nika Shahkarami, a seventeen-year-old girl who had disappeared on 22 September, only for her body to show up in a morgue a week later? We learned she was an ethnic Lur, born in Luristan. We knew she loved painting, studied in an art high school and worked in a café. We knew her parents, like millions of Iranians, had moved in search of a better life to Karaj, the giant feeder town to the west of Tehran.

What of the twenty-three-year-old Hadis Najafi, killed in Karaj on 23 September? We knew she had a degree in textile design but, like most Iranian graduates, could not find a job in her field. She worked as a cashier in a restaurant. Videos leaked soon after her death showing her singing along to Sura Iskenderli, an Azerbaijan-born Turkish pop star.[2]

Bit and pieces, fragments – this was all we had to go on to piece a picture together of their lives, their personalities, their aspirations. The regime wasn't keen on us knowing more than that, running a massive campaign of misinformation. They weren't protesters, the regime claimed, but people who had fallen from a roof or been killed by unidentified gunmen. It intimidated families and warned them of severe reprisals if they dared to tell the media the truth about their loved ones. Only the bravest overcame such fears.

Hadis's siter, Afsoon Najafi, spoke to the Prague-based *Radio Farda* to confirm that her sister had told her family she was joining the protests and had been killed.[3]

But even the sympathetic media, often based abroad, cared much more about protesters' deaths than their lives before September 2022. Who were these young men and women whose courage astonished the world? Why were teenagers putting their lives on the line to speak up against this brutal regime? More importantly, what did they want? What sort of Iran were they after?

If you want to understand the new brewing revolution in Iran, you have to find a way of answering these questions.

Revolutions are usually analysed by looking at their intellectuals – grafting ideology onto a mass movement. We pore over Thomas Paine to grasp the American Revolution, grapple with Voltaire and Rosseau to understand the French Revolution, read Frantz Fanon to come to terms with the Algerian Revolution. But ideologues don't make revolutions. Ordinary people do. Writing about the Russian Revolution, Leon Trotsky stated: 'The most indubitable feature of a revolution is the direct interference of the masses in historical events… The history of a revolution is for us first of all a history of the forcible entrance of the masses into the realm of rulership over their own destiny.'

But ordinary people don't frequently write tomes; they leave little in the written record for journalists and later historians to scrutinise. How do we uncover the motivations and ideas of the many thousands who came out to make history, including the few who sacrificed their lives for it? As the world attempted to understand the new Iranian revolution of 2022–23, many pundits came with readymade answers, comparing the movement to the 1979 revolution or the 2011 Arab Spring. If you watched prime-time TV experts in the West, you could be forgiven for thinking you were watching a rerun of some previous protest wave; so few sought to understand the new Iranian movement. But if the new Iranian revolution so far lacks its own *The Rights of Man*, it has something perhaps even more powerful: the thoughts of a teen-age girl who gave her life for the cause of Women, Life, Freedom. Her joy, her anger and her desire to live stand as a manifesto in their own right.

Sarina Esmayilzadeh was sixteen years old when on 23 September 2022 the Islamic Republic's security forces beat her to death under a rain of batons. Like thousands of people who came out all over Iran that day, she had joined the protests following the death of Mahsa Amini. The protest marched through Karaj's Mehrshahr neighbourhood, famed for the Pearl Palace, a former Pahlavi residence shaped like a batoid fish. It was on the same night, somewhere on the streets of the same neighbourhood, that Hadis Najafi met her death too. Sarina might have also been one of the many whose lives were reduced to a name, a few pictures and a handful of biographical facts. From the news reports, we knew which high school she went to, we knew her father had passed away in 2013, we knew she was living with her brother and her severely sick mother.

But Sarina had left behind more than others. Like many of her fellow Gen Z Iranians, she was an avid user of social media platforms. On them, she documented the vicissitudes of adolescence, her hopes and anxieties for the future and her daily routine. These posts were her public diary, a place to tell her story of growing up in a country where so much of basic life could be forbidden. Although they were created months before the protests kicked off, although they are often not political in nature, Sarina's reflections elucidate why so many of her generation are willing to risk their lives for change.

* * *

The multi-talented Sarina wrote poetry, made videos, drew impressively and loved dancing and curating music. In January 2022, a few months before her sixteenth birthday, she created a YouTube channel. In the channel's description, you could already hear her fun and eager voice: 'Hey, hey, I am still at the beginning so I can't say I am a blogger yet. But here I am anyways. Oh, before I forget, for the love of God, please SUBSCRIBE.'[4]

In April, just as a new Iranian calendar year was starting, she opened a channel on Telegram, a messaging and social media app popular in Iran, to share her writings. Her first post consisted of grumbling about her aunt and two pictures of her with a mask on, a reminder of the Covid-19 pandemic that had ripped through Iran. In May, she started posting her vlogs on YouTube. In August, she launched three new channels on Telegram: one for quotes, one for images and one for music. Between the five channels across Telegram and YouTube, her creativity shone through, illuminating both the delights and difficulties of Iranian teenagerhood.

Sarina was unique; she had no intention of being the voice of a generation. But anyone who knows Iranian teenagers instantly recognises a few shared traits. For myself, her way of speaking and her interests reminded me of two of my cousins in Tehran. She spoke in the same annoyingly English-afflicted Persian, starting her videos with a long '*guyssss*' in English. She listened to the same Persian rap and Western alternative rock songs. She was so consciously *cool* – especially compared to the teens of my generation. Her dreams, and the obstacles to them, resonated with me.

The most basic facts about past and present of women who live in Muslim-majority countries have long been subject to political manipulation, borrowed as tropes to score this or that point in Washington DC or in the ivory towers of Western universities. Pictures of mini skirt-wearing Iranian or Afghan women are instrumentalised to justify Western intervention in the Middle East by the hawks, while some nominally left-wing doves assert, against all evidence, that these women constitute a privileged elite, and the majority of Iranian women choose to live restricted lives.

These hackneyed pseudo-debates seem laughable from the perspective of a sixteen-year-old girl in Karaj in 2022. Sarina doesn't fit easy categories. Yes, she loves Western music but she is so unmistakably Iranian, in her mannerisms, in her over-the-top Persianate sentimentalism. She is not an 'elite' of any sort and seems to come from an ordinary family, sharing the economic anxieties of most Iranians, eating the same pizza and *qorme sabzi* (a meat and kidney bean stew cooked with fresh herbs), living in the same kind of middle-class apartment. Like most women, she hates compulsory Hijab and loves showing off her hair in her videos. But she is briefly seen visiting a Muslim shrine and hangs out with friends with a variety of Hijab or non-Hijab styles. More than anything, she's worried about her future in a country where 24% of young people are unemployed and inflation is spiralling out of control.[5] She's afraid of life under a regime that seems to revel in its utter contempt for young women.

Sarina's first vlog, posted on 16 May, recounts a one-day trip to Kashan, a gorgeous ancient city midway between Tehran and Isfahan.[6] Showcasing her style, she edits her observations of the trip with scenes of Gus Fring from *Breaking Bad* and the theme song from *Curb Your Enthusiasm*. In the car, she can be seen mouthing the words to Hozier's 'Take Me to Church', which later led to the Iranian regime-controlled outlets claiming she was under irreligious influence of the Irish singer-songwriter. In a soulful tribute shortly after her death, Hozier himself shared a video of Sarina singing his song and tweeted: 'We talk about freedoms with no understanding of what it means to pay the ultimate price in fighting for it. This brave girl was only sixteen years in the world.'[7] In other videos, she uses 'That's All She Wrote' by Eminem and 'Sometimes (Backwood)' by the Brooklyn-based Gigi Perez.

These Western songs made the headlines but Sarina also used many Iranian artists in her videos. There was one from the pioneering Tehran-born rapper Sohrab M.J. even though many considered him a regime sympathiser, especially after he attended a book launch by a pro-Khamenei propagandist in 2018.[8] There were also a couple of lines from 'Khafan', a tune from the musician Ho3ein Rahmati, hailing from Mashhad, who had been arrested and jailed in 2017 on grounds of his music insulting the authorities. *Khafan* is an untranslatable Persian neologism, belonging to a new vocabulary that has emerged in contemporary Iran, unbeknown to the older generations. It means something between 'cool' and 'awesome'. It's the perfect word for Sarina's vibes.

Sarina was by no means a convinced activist or ideologue, but like most teenagers, she rebelled against school, grown-ups and all authority. In Kashan's Rosewater Museum, she longs to see the fabled Damask rose flowers used to make the potion but is bored of the tour guide 'talking her nonsense'. As she goes underground to see an ancient subterranean town, she makes a reference to 'the tunnel dug by Helsinki and the Professor,' characters from the Spanish crime drama *La Casa de Papel* (*Money Heist* on Netflix).

Documenting her first ever attempt at make-up, we see her make a mess of her eyeliner.[9] In another video, introducing Karaj's glitzy Mehrdad Mall, she gets annoyed when staff stop her from filming. She then disobeys them and continues to film inside the shops, lamenting how empty they are and making fun of a store called Tehran Home for wanting to be an IKEA so badly but failing. She almost shrieks in excitement when she sees a store selling Haribo-style gummy sweets.[10]

As you can see, Sarina didn't languish in a tragic tale of repression. In one of her most touching videos, on 24 June, she portrays her life for a few days after her final exam. In the video's description, she wrote: 'Helloooo, I am here after so long. I always thought my life is so routine and boring but since I started this vlog, I am thinking, noooo, it's not so bad either. My life is cool in its own ways.'[11]

She took joy in drinking her coffee-flavoured *Istak,* an alcohol-free beer. It was summer and she was bursting with life; she loved playing volleyball with her friends, playing football in a Dortmund FC Jersey, searching videos on YouTube for 'how to do 180 degree splits'. Now with her exams over, she spoke excitedly about the places she wanted to go, films to watch, books to read. She wanted to make the most of life, grab it by the horns.

But she can't live a carefree life, at least not under the regime. In other videos, she displays her political and social consciousness – criticising the regime for the poor conservation of a historic mosque in Kashan. She is outraged when she sees a graffiti reading: 'Best job for women is to be a housewife and raise kids.' Sarina tells her audience: 'You see what culture our country has!' adding 'what the fuck' in English. Passing a bookstore, she shows a special interest in a portrait of Albert Camus, declaring her affinity with the melancholic French existentialist.

Sarina had no way of escaping politics because her lifestyle, despite being ordinary for young women anywhere else in the world, was subject to suppression by the regime. In any of her seemingly mundane videos, she could be seen breaking an endless list of rules imposed by the regime: appearing without Hijab, singing out loud, listening to forbidden domestic and foreign music, hanging out with people of the opposite sex and expressing her opinions openly. As a woman she couldn't go to a football stadium, smoke shisha or ride a bicycle publicly. Even if she had been content to live under all these restrictions, Iran's utter economic collapse meant that her generation could hardly hope for a comfortable life, let alone a free one.

She understood the stakes. In a video posted on 22 May, entitled 'Ramblings of Iranian youth', she delivers twelve minutes of her ideas about the predicament of her fellow young Iranians.[12] If her other videos were a window into her life and her aspirations, 'Ramblings' is something of a manifesto. Sitting in her room in an Adventure Time-themed sweatshirt, her bookcases filled with exam guides, her desk littered with empty soda cans, Sarina departs from her usual cheerful videos by offering a sombre commentary on the state of the nation.

'Hey guys!' she starts 'Today, I come to you with a different video. I want to ask something from all of you: you who are twenty-five, you who are twenty. Let us all imagine a sixteen-year-old teenager, living in the current conditions of Iran. Let's then talk about the concerns and joys of a teenager.'

She informs us that these aren't just her opinions, but her thoughts after talking to her friends and families. She tells us 'the most important concern' of a teenager is studying because it's the sole pathway to a good job. But teenagers today, she says, face multiple obstacles on this path, and some are insurmountable.

'Our country, Iran,' she says. 'We've all tasted its problems. Some of us more, some of us less. But we all know what shape Iran is in today. What can people expect from their own country?

Prosperity! Well, our economic conditions are terrible, our cultural conditions are terrible, and our authenticity is being ruined. A bunch of limitations are especially severe on women, like the compulsory Hijab. Or all that is banned for women but not for men.'

But Sarina's criticism is not limited to the policy of the regime. She goes to the heart of patriarchal social structures in the country and says: 'When it comes to freedom, our discussion gets dark. Because freedom is something that so many Iranian families have deprived their daughters of. In Iranian families, a little boy doesn't need to tell anyone when he goes outside to play with his friends, doesn't need to get permission from anyone. But little girls are told that they have to either go to their friend's house or play in their own house. And even this is not an option for all girls. I've seen girls whose mom doesn't allow them to go to their friend's house and they can only play at school.'

'This is what's painful,' she adds. 'This is what bothers me. This is the freedom that is a dream in the heart of us youth.'

Sarina may have never left Iran, but she knew that beyond its borders, young people enjoy opportunities which she was denied.

'It's not like twenty years ago anymore,' she says. 'When we didn't know any teenagers other than those in Iran. We see people dying out of hunger in Ethiopia, and also those who are having the time of their lives in Berlin. And human beings naturally always look at the those with the better conditions and want to get there...You think, "Why am I not like the teenagers living in New York or Los Angeles?"'

'I have always thought to myself: why?' she continues, repeating a line familiar to many young Iranians. 'Why should my life to be so different from theirs? Just because I was born in Iran? My concerns now have to be so different from theirs. We are stuck on the first level of the pyramid: food, clothing and housing.'

'Our brain is so preoccupied with these three basic things,' she asserts. 'Our mind can't even get thinking about higher goals.'

Sarina, at sixteen years old, knew her generation couldn't expect more than patriarchal rule, political suppression and a bitter struggle just to make ends meet. In other words, she wanted Women, Life, Freedom. So when a movement raised this as their banner, she joined it and stood proudly on the frontlines, demanding change.

Her writing channel on Telegram, entitled *My Whole Universe*, had been mostly dedicated to poetic musings about life, often written in a cryptic fashion, familiar to the Persian literary tradition.[13] Some had a romantic side. On 14 September, she had written a poem: 'What were the colour of those eyes? Blue? I don't know! Maybe purple! My lips were hot. I asked him to close his eyes. I kissed him and felt the long and curly eyelashes.'

But on 16 September, the day Mahsa died, the tone changed. Sarina first reacted with a simple post: 'Mood: Why is everything shit everywhere?' A forlorn poem followed on the same day, 'A cry that can't find a mouth'; its closing lines read, 'Eyes that can't see, a sky that has no colours, an autumn that sees no rain and an end that sees no end.'

But her despair soon turned into a righteous anger, buoyed by the infectious courage shown by thousands during those days. On

20 September she posted a picture of demonstrators confronted by the police with a telling caption: 'The Islamic Republic of Iran'. But 'of' had been crossed out – it now read 'The Islamic Republic vs Iran'. Sarina knew which side she was on. The two posts before her eventual killing were short, one sentence each, each of them three words in Persian. On 20 September, she asked: 'Could it really happen?' On 21 September, she wrote: 'I feel homesick in my homeland.'

On her image channel on Telegram, which had been previously mostly full of artsy-looking intimate pictures of young men and women, political photographs started appearing on 21 September.[14] On this day, she posted an iconic picture of a Hijab-less girl looking on as her comrade threw stones at the police. She also posted pictures of women burning their Hijabs on sticks and of a University of Tehran demonstration with the slogan: 'If we don't join each other, they'll finish us off one by one.' On her music channel, she had been doing a popular online thirty-day song challenge.[15] Her last post came on 22 September. According to the challenge, she was to post 'a song that makes you happy' on Day 9. Instead of posting a song, she wrote: 'Now, how I could post a song that makes one happy?' A day later, Sarina was killed as she joined her brothers and sisters on the street.

This was Sarina's revolution now. Following her tragic death, as her name spread like wildfire around the world, the state media claimed she had never even been to a demonstration and had actually committed suicide by jumping off a roof. Her mother and her purported neighbours appeared on TV, confirming this was the case.

But for Iranians, this simply verified that Sarina was a martyr. As the uprising mourned its fallen, the regime concocted these implausible narratives for each person they killed, starting from Mahsa herself who, the regime claimed, had died from pre-existing medical problems. Since the state broadcaster was notorious for extracting forced confessions, frequently obtained through intimidation or even torture, no one bought its story. And Sarina's voice couldn't be stifled by her death, no matter how hard the regime tried. Her thoughts and ideas, on Telegram and on YouTube, revealed her hope for a better country, for a free Iran. Her voice cut through all the noise and was heard by Iranians across the world.

* * *

One of the most resonant political slogans in Iran is the demand for 'a normal life'. It made it to the new movement's anthem *Baraye* and it even has an echo in the very name Women, *Life*, Freedom. The slogan might seem naïve, or even too modest – what's a 'normal' life anyway? But in Sarina's life, and in her frustrations at her country, what 'normal' means is obvious: a life where she can sing, dance, style her hair without worrying about the regime's Guidance Patrol cracking down on her. It's a life where young people can expect to pursue their interests and enjoy successful careers. It's a world in which a lot more things are possible.

This simple-sounding slogan is actually a radical reversal of the 1979 revolution. Coming as they did in the tail-end of the Global Sixties, the '79 revolutionaries were true children of their time: Like the Red Guards of Shanghai, students of Paris and urban guerrillas of Montevideo, they were on an utopian quest to tear everything down and rebuild it from the ground up. All that was solid had to melt into air. Khomeini's Islamic Republic was the logical conclusion – setting itself against liberal democracy and state socialism in equal measure. Its philosopher-king and its uncompromising opposition to other ideological systems persuaded many would-be revolutionaries of its merits, even those who should have known better.

The 2022 revolution for a 'normal life' aimed for the exact opposite. These revolutionaries didn't want to remake Iran in their own image; they wanted an Iranian government made in the image of Iranian people in their everyday joys and long-term aspirations. They didn't want Iran to be a laboratory for a revolutionary social experiment, but sought an end to the decades-long experiment Iranians still suffer under. They wanted to be able to say Iran was a 'normal country'.

In this sense, Iran's new revolutionaries resemble a return to the older tradition of the Iranian quest for democracy and civil rights, embodied in the Persian Constitutional Revolution of 1906. Paradoxically, however, the Iranian quest for normality and democracy appears quite revolutionary in 2022. As authoritarianism's star is in the ascendant across the globe, Iranians are knocking on the door of history, aiming to take their country back and jolt the world's political imagination.

Sarina just wanted to be a normal teenager, like teens in London, Berlin or New York. But this was a revolutionary demand. It's likely she never heard an old Irish socialist song, penned by the revolutionary James Connolly, which declares proudly 'Our demands most moderate are, we only want the earth.' But its spirit beat in her, as it beats in all those fighting for a decent life for all.

Epilogue

What's next?

I'm writing this in July 2023. By the time you read these pages, the Islamic Republic might be a very different place. This book might document a flash of hope – a revolt against the ongoing catastrophe of the regime – extinguished too soon to secure lasting change. Or it could testify to the inaugural scene of a new revolution, the beginnings of a thorough transformation.

I once joked with a persistent inquirer that predicting Iran's future is the easiest thing to do. Your guess is as good as any expert's. Time and time again, Iranians have upturned the world's expectations – and they show no signs of stopping.

I can't predict the future. But Iran is clearly approaching a fork in the road. I *can* offer a prognosis of the path Iran might take.

Now, in July 2023, the 2022–23 uprising has reached a lull. But the fundamental contradictions of Iranian society organised under the regime – the clash of ideals and power between opposed social forces – rumble on, threatening to break out into open conflict. Slowly, painfully, but unmistakably, Iran is turning a page in its history. What will the next chapter look like?

Dual Crises

It has long become axiomatic to observers of Iran that the Islamic Republic is suffering from dual crises of legitimacy and competency. Founded at the tail-end of an era of global revolutionary upheavals, the Islamic Republic of 1979 claimed to offer a genuine alternative to both dominant models of its time: capitalism and state socialism. Its founders had pledged to build a moral Islamic polity that would serve as a beacon for the rest of the world. Theirs was, they often claimed, the 'most people-oriented revolution in history'. Just over four decades on, even the regime's own elites no longer believe in those founding ideals. The Islamic Republic has manifestly failed to offer an appealing political, economic or social model. If the pioneering generation had pledged to construct an economy for the 'oppressed', Iran today is an unabashedly oligarchic capitalist state with obscene inequality and a small super-rich class, often consisting of regime-linked families, proudly brandishing their Porsche cars and Givenchy bags. If the revolution had promised to bring 'freedom', Iranians of 2024 can only bemoan its lack. Many of the revolutionary generation now openly lament that they had made the 1979 revolution to bring about political and civic freedoms and ended up under a more repressive regime, robbed even of their earlier social freedoms. If the 1979 revolution had promised 'independence', Iran of 2024 stands out for its international isolation, crippled by sanctions on par with those imposed upon Putin's Russia and North Korea. To make things worse, not only has the Islamic Republic not realised any of its original lofty ideals, it also fails any basic test of state competence.

For the past few decades, many of the regime's elite have well understood these twin crises and tried to address them. Those who aimed to overcome the crisis of legitimacy by making the Islamic Republic more democratic and representative formed the reformist faction of official politics. Those who preferred authoritarian rule that could oversee economic growth and competent state functions formed the technocratic faction. The former was best represented by President Mohammad Khatami (1997–2005) while the latter was best represented by presidents Ali Akbar Hashemi Rafsanjani (1989–97) and Hassan Rouhani (2013–17). But neither of these political factions was able to truly rule the roost in the Islamic Republic. In 2023 reformists find themselves banned from almost any political activity and in many cases imprisoned, while technocrats have been politically sidelined. In power, neither successfully managed to stand up to the entrenched interests of the Islamic Republic itself. Both factions have now lost the popular support that they mobilised for their electoral victories, nor do they have strong social movements behind them.

Instead one man has emerged as the all-powerful decision-maker of the Islamic Republic: Khamenei. Ever since he assumed the position in 1989, the Supreme Leader often flitted between the two main political factions of the Islamic Republic. Constantly looking to strengthen his personal hold on power, he ultimately found the surest base of support in the IRGC, the militia established to help Iran fight the Iraqi invasion during the 1980s but which mushroomed into a powerful political and economic powerhouse afterwards. It has long been clear that reformist democratisation or technocratic reform will endanger the IRGC's tight grip over Iran, and they are unwilling to relinquish the influence they've gained through Khamenei. With the help of this praetorian guard, Khamenei has succeeded in eliminating all opponents.

Yet the Supreme Leader has also been careful not to cede power to the IRGC. Although the powerful militia now controls most of the Iranian economy and armed forces, it still hasn't seized the key levers of the state. Whenever IRGC figures have tried to run for the presidency, Khamenei has used his control of various state bodies to block them. The Guardian Council, whose twelve members are all selected by Khamenei or his appointees, has consistently thrown out the candidacy of IRGC figures for presidency. Locked out of the main electoral contests, there's no incentive for differing factions within the IRGC to fight among themselves. So long as the Supreme Leader is around, they all agree to toe his line. This unholy alliance of the Great Dictator and his militia will likely only come undone with Khamenei's death.

Two Futures

The dictator's physical demise, or a cataclysm that removes him from power, is almost guaranteed to lead to an unravelling of the untenable status quo. Many analysts are now preoccupied with a simple question: who will replace Khamenei as Supreme Leader? But this question misses the point. The unique institution of the Supreme Leader, which is reserved by the constitution for clerics, is unlikely to survive in its current form after Khamenei. He has ensured that no clerical figure has the necessary charisma or political capital to emerge as a strong Supreme Leader. All the potential candidates have long been sidelined. It is likely that whoever is picked to be the next Supreme Leader will be beholden to one faction within the regime, incapable of exercising power independently. There might even be a constitutional change to get rid of the position altogether. Here's the real question about Iran's future once Khamenei is gone: who will emerge as the victor in the struggle for power across the IRGC, including its internal factions, and Iran's social mass movements?

It will be a pitched battle between two poles: one consisting of the IRGC, the ambitious men who control the guns and the butter, the other consisting of the men and women at the heart of this book, whose resources are bravery and determination.

The latter lack organisation, so in the immediate post-Khamenei period they will be the underdogs. They will have to fight hard for a credible democratic alternative, one that can unify the millions in the country who want change. But even if the IRGC, or a single leader from its ranks, comes to power, it is highly likely that they will put an end to some of the worst policies of the current regime. As the guards are currently the enforcers of Khamenei's regime, it might be hard to imagine them changing their colours. But the persistence of the dual crises and bankruptcy of the ruling ideology means that it is very likely to be buried with Khamenei. Conscious of the persistent patriotism of Iranians, they are likely to reinvent themselves as Iranian nationalists. A charismatic military figure or group of generals taking charge and granting some of the most popular social demands, while restricting political freedom, is a plausible scenario. Already many high-ranking IRGC figures, including some I have spoken to myself, privately muse about such possibilities. In this Iran, people could dress how they like, eat and drink what they like, and enjoy the films, books and songs they want, as long as they don't cross certain red lines politically. Women will be able to pursue careers freely and travel without a male guardian's permission. More importantly, this Iran would drop its hostility towards the US and Israel, abandoning military and nuclear plans that have turned Iran into a pariah state, economically enfeebled by decades of sanctions. It would be tough for Iranian democrats to swallow but such a regime would likely satisfy many Iranians who took to the streets in 2022 and 2023. For a few years, at least.

But only a few years. No matter what comes after Khamenei, Iran's formidable mass movements will continue to fight for Women, Life, Freedom: the fullest democracy and social, economic, environmental and gender justice. Those who paid for progress with prison sentences are not going to be satisfied with half-measures. We've now heard the voices of Iranian women and men fighting for causes that resonate across the world. They are no longer simply fighting for rights and freedoms that the West takes for granted; they are fighting for a just society that the West seems content to let slip away. The end of theocratic rule by Khamenei will undoubtedly bring some welcome respite. But their struggles will go on. As always with revolutions, the true battle starts tomorrow.

Acknowledgements

I wrote this book for a simple reason: because Novin Doostdar, Oneworld's publisher, asked me to. How could I pass up the opportunity to write about the awe-inspiring struggles of my compatriots? I am grateful to him and his partner-in-crime, Juliet Mabey, for giving me the honour of telling the story of the women and men of my country, whom I've admired all my life.

In Rida Vaquas, I had the dreamiest editor I could ask for. Who else could be equally conversant in Rosa Luxemburg, stories from Islamic lore and twenty-first-century youth culture? If this book is relatively mistake-free or readable, it's all thanks to her. For the book's publicity, I am grateful to Kate Appleton at

Oneworld, and Dana Kaye, Hailey Dezort and their colleagues at Kaye Publicity in Chicago.

My mother, Mitra Mansouri, was my first feminist hero and the first activist I came to admire. I am grateful to her and my sister Parastoo Azizi for all they've taught me and all their love.

I was writing this book while also preparing for my doctoral defence. I am grateful to my advisors Zachary Lockman, Arang Keshavarzian and Sara Pursley as well as my external committee members Lior Sternfeld and Ervand Abrahamian for patiently working with me through the dissertation and for granting me a PhD. My path to a PhD was paved with the support of so many professors and colleagues that are too many to name. I am especially indebted to Ato Quayson, Anna Shternshis, Antonela Arhin, Jeffrey Kopstein and Ruth Marshall at the University of Toronto; Sebastian Conrad, Nora Lafi and and Nadin Heé at the Free University of Berlin and Ayse Baltacioglu-Brammer at NYU.

This book owes a lot to my wife Ayse Lokmanoglu. From the very outset, there is scarcely any idea in this book which I didn't first run through with her. The organisation of the book into its current chapter structure was mostly her idea. As I've said elsewhere, I know that I might never be as good a scholar as she is, but I will always try to be as good a partner to her as she is to me. Thanks to Ayse, I've also found a new family in the beautiful city of Mersin, Turkey and, across the Mediterranean, in Cyprus. I am grateful to my in-laws and to Ayse's extended family.

In New York City, Etan Nechin and Didi Tal remain indispensable friends. I can't imagine a writing life without their presence. Just as I started writing this book, they also brought a new joy to our lives in form of a beautiful baby boy. I write with the hope that one day I can take these friends to Iran and show them the homeland I so miss.

Like much else in my life, I discussed many ideas of this book with Negar Mottahedeh. The first chapter of this book is inspired by Negar's amazing book, *The Whisper Tapes: Kate Millet in Iran*. As I am in the process of translating this book to Persian, I have the pleasure of living both with Negar's friendship and her enviable prose.

I first got to know Bachar Halabi and Yara Asmar after they read my first book, *The Shadow Commander*. They have since become dear friends and I constantly rely on their wisdom for understanding our crazy yet lovable region. I am also grateful to Danny Postel in Chicago for his friendship and for the excellent feedback he gave on my first book. He is also now an editor at the amazing *New Lines Magazine* and I am so glad I get to write for him sometimes.

Since my good friend Holly Dagres moved to Washington DC, I have a very good reason to visit often. Since I first met her many years ago in Cairo, we have both crossed continents many times but our friendship remains solid and I am so grateful for her continued friendship and wisdom and all the laughs we get to have together.

At the United States Holocaust Memorial Museum, my colleagues Andrea Bertrand, Tad Stahnke, Katie Doyle and Ilana Weinberg regularly brighten my screen and make my day. The honour of being involved with them in such a worthy endeavour enriches my life. I am grateful to Maziar Bahari, my editor at *IranWire*, for introducing me to the museum and for giving me the opportunity to write about the homeland we both love so much.

In Toronto, one of my previous homes, I am still in touch with many friends. Constance Dilley helped shepherd me into a life of letters and I am grateful for her enduring friendship and counsel. I also dearly miss the Toronto trio of Alex and Jim Conchie and Lynne Thorndycraft and our many conversations about life, Canadian politics, the history of Bolshevik Russia and everything in between. I was always touched by how much care Jim, Lynne and Alex showed toward Iran and the struggles of its people for liberty. I thought of their internationalist spirit as I wrote this book.

Among the figures I've described in this book, Fatemeh Haghighatjoo is someone I have long admired, years before I met her in person. The fact that I now also get to work with her and call her a friend is a true privilege.

For their friendship, and for the basic act of tolerating me, I am indebted to my friends Rohan Advani, Loubna Mrie and Verena Walther. Here's hoping I get to see more of them now that this book is over!

Iranian civil society has long been a lodestar of my life and much of this book is a tribute to it. Far away from home, in the United States, I am honoured to be working with Firuzeh

Mahmoudi and her colleagues at United4Iran, as we strive to support the civil society our hearts beat for. In the short few years of knowing her, I've learnt so much from Firuzeh that I sometimes can't believe it's only been a few years. We must have known each other in another life.

I wrote this book not as a disinterested observer but as a passionate supporter of my people's quest for freedom. Nothing reminded me more sharply of the high stakes as the lives of my friends and family members in Tehran and other cities in the country, affected every day by the events described in this book. Ultimately, this book belongs to them. I can't wait for the time when we can take back our country and I can embrace them in our homeland again.

Notes

1 Freedom is Global: The Fight Against Compulsory Hijab

1 *Etemad* Newspaper, 18 September 2022.

2 *Jamaran News*, 16 September 2022, https://tinyurl.com/r99f3p8s.

3 A widely distributed video showed the fire: https://www.youtube.com/watch?v=XrdLDqkFrSQ. Iranian officials claimed that no such arson had taken place.

4 Interview with author, April 2023.

5 Kelly J. Shannon, 'Four decades of smoldering discontent among Iranian women is erupting', *Washington Post*, 26 September 2022.

6 Mina Avanj, 'The Position of Women in Imam Khomeini's View', imam-khomeini.ir: https://tinyurl.com/4jhw8rxf.

7 Mina Avanj, 'The Position of Women in Imam Khomeini's View', https://tinyurl.com/4jhw8rxf.

8 Speaking to Radio Farda in February 2019, Amiri gave a detailed account of that historic interview: https://tinyurl.com/ycxukjrm.

9 *Ayandegan* newspaper, 6 February, 1979.

10 The episode and this exchange is recounted in Chapter 3 of Janet Afary and Kevin B. Anderson, *Foucault and the Iranian Revolution: Gender and the Seductions of Islamism*. Chicago: University of Chicago Press, 2005.

11 As recounted by Nima Namdari in this article for *Meydaan-e Zanan*, first published in 2007, now available here: https://tinyurl.com/4fjh7trz.

12 From the collected works of Ayatollah Khomeini, hosted on farsi.rouhollah.ir. This comes from Volume 6: https://tinyurl.com/hnnkrxbv.

13 As quoted in an article by Fariba Nazari, published by Iran Transition Council, https://tinyurl.com/2vyzx9ry.

14 Ibid. https://tinyurl.com/2swyppwt.

15 Millet's trip is the focus of the extraordinary volume by Iranian-American scholar Negar Mottahedeh, *Whisper Tapes: Kate Millet in Iran*. Redwood: Stanford University Press, 2019. Much of this chapter is inspired by this book.

16 For an excellent account of the events of March 1979 see Mahnaz Matin and Naser Mohajer, *Khizesh-e Zanan-e Iran dar Esfand 1357*. Cologne: Nashre Noqte, 2013.

17 Kateh Vafadari's interview with the author, August 2023.

18 https://shahrvand.com/archives/83649.

19 https://www.aasoo.org/fa/articles/1767.

20 *Kayhan* newspaper, 11 March 1979.

21 Kelly, Shannon, *US Foreign Policy and Muslim Women's Human Rights*. Philadelphia: University of Pennsylvania Press, 2017, p. 62.

22 https://www.tribunezamaneh.com/archives/145007.

23 Shujai, Mitra, 'How the Hijab became mandatory at the start of the Revolution', *Deutsche Welle* Persian, 4 January 2014, https://tinyurl.com/4nt2tykf.

24 https://www.aparat.com/v/qay4T.

25 'Hijab law from felony to misdemeanour', Resalat-News.com, https://tinyurl.com/3v78cksu.

26 https://www.youtube.com/watch?v=WELjXQdjzug.

27 When she passed away in 2019, I wrote her obituary for the *New York Times*: https://www.nytimes.com/2019/11/01/world/azam-taleghani-dead.html.

28 Interview with Sahar Rezazadeh and Masih Alinejad, in Arseh Sevom, https://tinyurl.com/4bt2c8sv.

29 https://www.facebook.com/StealthyFreedom/.

30 Article in *Asr Iran*: https://tinyurl.com/3673pjzx.

31 In 2018, Masih retold her life story – see Masih Alinejad, *Wind in My Hair*. New York, Boston and London: Little, Brown and Company, 2018.

32 Article in Persian-language Radio Farda, https://tinyurl.com/nhjvdp82.

33 BBC News Persian, March 2018, https://tinyurl.com/5y25f989.

34 https://tinyurl.com/bdhs5epn.

35 https://tinyurl.com/yakbf3cm.

36 Asef Bayat, *Life As Politics: How Ordinary People Can Change the Middle East*. Redwood: Stanford University Press, 2013.

2 Yes, I Am a Woman: The Fight for Women's Rights

1 Article by Arash Azizi for *Independent* Persian edition, https://tinyurl.com/288r4653.

2 BBC News Persian, 16 March 2023, https://tinyurl.com/4afsmwt9.

3 Interview with the author, 15 June 2023.

4 In 2003, Hoora, an academic journal in Iran dedicated to Women's Studies, published a full legal history of the episode: https://tinyurl.com/2p95d6cx.

5 Interview with Faeze Hashemi, Iranian Students' News Agency, https://tinyurl.com/5t4sez3d.

6 Online archive of Noushin Ahmadi Khorasani's writings, 12 May 2010, https://tinyurl.com/5anejjbm.

7 https://www.nobelprize.org/prizes/peace/2003/ebadi/facts/.

8 'Shirin Ebadi at Mehrabad Airport,' Iranian Students' News Agency, https://tinyurl.com/yj28ynwe.

9 https://www.radiozamaneh.com/264904/.

10 https://www.tribunezamaneh.com/archives/185300.

11 'Police Attack on Women's Day Rally', *Deutsche Welle* Persian, 8 March 2006, https://tinyurl.com/y3f3bzv3.

12 'Hafte-Tir Gathering', BBC News Persian, https://tinyurl.com/3hsb83re.

13 In 2007, Ahmadi Khorasani wrote a book-length history of the movement as one of its main founders: https://tinyurl.com/56wu74kk.

14 https://www.youtube.com/watch?v=EOFPsZZV9-g&t=2s&ab_channel=NasimAmiri.

3 We Want a Union! The Fight for the Labour Movement

1 https://www.youtube.com/watch?v=iNzDqYHQmyY.

2 https://www.youtube.com/watch?v=WfXM-LXgoDw.

3 https://www.facebook.com/watch/?v=541273830676526.

4 https://ir.voanews.com/a/strike-iran-protest-mahsa-amini-bandare-abbas/6854513.html.

5 Reported in *IranWire*, December 2022, https://tinyurl.com/4jj3848j.

6 https://www.radiozamaneh.com/744229/.

7   Reported in *Iran Wire*, December 2022, https://tinyurl.com/3f4v2u6y.

8   https://www.radiozamaneh.com/744710/.

9   https://www.akhbar-rooz.com/183375/1401/09/15/.

10 https://www.akhbar-rooz.com/134574/1400/09/17/.

11 https://kargareirani.blogsky.com/1398/12/18/post-271/.

12 https://kargareirani.blogsky.com/1398/06/15/post-241/.

13 http://asre-nou.net/1384/day/4/m-etesab.html.

14 https://www.radiofarda.com/a/a-version-on-mansour-osanlou-labor-activist/32178383.html.

15 In 2017, on the anniversary of the December 2005 strike, the Association of Workers' Rights Defenders published a brief history of the union: https://melliun.org/iran/149088.

16 https://www.youtube.com/watch?v=gUZcR_dzons&ab_channel=azhir1979.

17 https://www.youtube.com/watch?v=XGHSPZPtW3s.

18 Reported by *Iran Wire*. https://tinyurl.com/58h3rran.

19 https://cpiran.org/2019/9/maghalat/page2.html.

20 https://iranhr.net/fa/articles/4649/.

21 https://davtalab.org/2021/907/.

22 http://www.iran-chabar.de/article.jsp?essayId=28817.

23 http://www.chiran-echo.com/2440.htm.

24 https://melliun.org/iran/14419.

25 Reported by *Tasnim News*, https://tinyurl.com/5d7pkm3f.

26 https://www.facebook.com/watch/?v=435802927288407.

27 https://www.youtube.com/watch?v=8P9pGUxBVoE.

28 I reported on the episode for *Iran Wire*: https://iranwire.com/en/features/65793/.

29 https://www.bbc.com/persian/iran-46954368.

30 https://www.radiofarda.com/a/haft-tapaeh-kian-pir-falak/32334633.html.

4 The Cheetah Who Died for the Revolution: The Fight for the Environment

1 https://twitter.com/PahlaviReza/status/1630581611765944322?s=20.
2 Reported by *Khabar Online*, https://tinyurl.com/499sb637.
3 Reported by Iranian Students' News Agency, https://tinyurl.com/murn7n7r.
4 *Arman-e Melli* newspaper, 9 November 2021.
5 Reported by Iranian Students' News Agency, https://tinyurl.com/29raptd9.
6 https://shiraz1400.ir/?p=2484.
7 Reported by the Islamic Republic News Agency, https://tinyurl.com/mrndcrhd.
8 From tasvirnet.com, https://tinyurl.com/5xz8da3n.
9 Reported by Iranian Students' News Agency, https://tinyurl.com/5986k2tx.
10 Before he was arrested, I wrote a hopeful profile of Madani for IranWire: https://iranwire.com/en/features/65054/.
11 Reported by *Deutsche Welle* Persian, https://tinyurl.com/4zwm78ay.
12 https://www.bbc.com/persian/iran-features-51549394.
13 https://ir.voanews.com/a/environmental-activists-imprisoned-in-iran/6980937.html.

5 We Accuse! The Fight for Freedom of Expression

1 https://www.instagram.com/p/CipXz4HsWgL/?img_index=1.
2 Reported by *Hamshahri* online, https://tinyurl.com/34c3453j.
3 https://www.instagram.com/p/CkwBqrkraMU/.
4 https://www.iranintl.com/202206016950.
5 Reported by *Deutsche Welle* Persian, https://tinyurl.com/5889wk5u.
6 https://www.iranintl.com/202212085996.

7 Reported by *Java* online, https://tinyurl.com/yc69hybd.

8 https://www.voanews.com/a/film-stars-call-for-release-of-jailed-iranian-actor-alidoosti-/6888492.html.

9 Reported by Peyke Iran, https://tinyurl.com/5ecyfm2d.

10 Reported by *Khabar* online, https://tinyurl.com/ynx5xj4d.

11 Video on Aparat. https://tinyurl.com/bdweuure.

12 Reported by *Khabar* online. https://tinyurl.com/2hc6fwcm.

13 Reported by Donya-e-Eqtesad. https://tinyurl.com/5925te37.

14 https://melliun.org/iran/179866.

15 Reported by *Khabar* online. https://tinyurl.com/3czsj7j5.

16 https://www.si.com/soccer/2018/06/23/carles-puyol-iran-tv-world-cup-hair-ban.

17 Reported by Asr Iran, https://tinyurl.com/ehcmxcrv.

18 Reported by Donya-e-Eqtesad, https://tinyurl.com/y8v59kn4.

19 Reported by *Eghtesad News*. https://tinyurl.com/4wkre62b.

20 https://www.bbc.com/news/world-middle-east-62205744.

21 https://farsi.rouhollah.ir/library/sahifeh-imam-khomeini/vol/6/page/354.

22 https://farsi.rouhollah.ir/library/sahifeh-imam-khomeini/vol/9/page/282.

23 In 2015, Mandanipour gave an oral history account of the story to BBC: https://www.bbc.com/persian/arts/2015/08/150806_l45_armenia_bus_mandanipor.

24 Their daughter, Parastoo Forouhar, later wrote a book about her parents from her German exile: https://www.parastou-forouhar.de/1868/.

25 Reported by Gooya News, https://tinyurl.com/2s3zbu9f.

26 Interview with Nasser Zarafshan, *Deutsche Welle* Persian, https://tinyurl.com/3r244bx4.

27 https://www.radiofarda.com/a/who-is-baktash-abtin-poet-who-died-in-prison/31645204.html.

28 https://bepish.org/node/7887.

29 https://www.zeitoons.com/107317.

30 http://baangnews.net/11746.

6 We Are All Iranians: The Fight For Freedom of Religion

1   https://kadivar.com/16486/.

2   https://www.radiofarda.com/a/32054153.html.

3   https://www.youtube.com/watch?v=90KD9_CfPyQ.

4   https://www.youtube.com/watch?v=9QoWUn1pXx.

5   https://www.cbsnews.com/chicago/news/iranian-protester-honored/.

6   https://www.youtube.com/watch?v=6S6m9JP97UU.

7   https://abdolhamid.net/persian/2013/05/11/165/.

8   Reported by Defenders of Human Rights Center, https://tinyurl.com/yc3r4nr5.

9   Reported by *Independent* Persian, https://tinyurl.com/bddrb98h.

10 https://www.humanrights-ir.org/detail/2461.

11 Reported by Tasnim News, https://tinyurl.com/c682bvux.

12 https://www.youtube.com/watch?v=eN63oauJEYA.

13 https://www.aparat.com/v/HCfjB.

14 https://www.youtube.com/watch?v=AR5XWqEQJVg.

15 https://www.bbc.com/persian/articles/cd1z99jjpxzo.

16 Reported by Tasnim News, https://tinyurl.com/2yya7xxc.

17 https://tinyurl.com/dvsr4tk5.

18 https://www.bbc.com/persian/iran/2015/10/150503_l44_revolutionary_injustice_bahai.

19 Reported by *IranWire*, https://tinyurl.com/msfwuzaz.

20 https://iranbahaipersecution.bic.org/fa/archive/aday-mhfl-mly-dwm-kh-hft-nfr-az-anan-dr-dy-1360-tyrbaran-shdnd.

21 https://news.bahai.org/human-rights/iran/yaran-special-report/
feature-articles/the-1991-memorandum-on-the-bahai-question.

22 https://www.bic.org/sites/default/files/pdf/rouhani_economic_letter_
booklet_final_web_version.pdf.

23 Together with Maziar Bahari, I made a film about Bahá'í experience
during apartheid which is available to watch online: https://iranwire.
com/en/special-features/64762/.

24 Reported by *IranWire*, https://tinyurl.com/bdd9n52f.

25 https://www.aparat.com/v/8QK5f.

26 https://www.zeitoons.com/8673.

27 Reported by *Deutsche Welle* Persian, https://tinyurl.com/msjdh7dk.

28 https://iranbahaipersecution.bic.org/fa/archive/karzar-ayran-bdwn-
nfrt-chra-w-chgwnh-tshkyl-shd.

29 https://www.bbc.com/persian/iran-44909976.

30 https://www.radiofarda.com/a/31242486.html.

31 https://www.iran-emrooz.net/index.php/news2/84139/.

32 https://iranwire.com/fa/features/626/.

33 https://www.ushmm.org/antisemitism/holocaust-denial-and-distor-
tion/holocaust-denial-antisemitism-iran/crime-and-denial.

7 Our Common Pain: The Fight for Refugee Rights

1 https://www.rferl.org/a/iran-job-restrictions-afghan-migrants/
32462715.html.

2 Reported by Farda News, https://tinyurl.com/3vpar8x2.

3 https://www.afintl.com/202209200185.

4 Reported by Radio France Internationale, Iran, https://tinyurl.com/
54zyt8kn.

5 https://www.bbc.com/persian/articles/c16xk7xj7wno.

6   Reported by Iran International, https://tinyurl.com/4kc97y5f.

7   https://www.hrw.org/news/2013/11/20/iran-afghan-refugees-and-migrants-face-abuse.

8   https://zantimes.com/fa/2022/10/22/racism-and-misogyny-the-plight-of-afghan-women-in-iran-2/.

9   https://meidaan.com/archive/68345.

10 Arash Nasr Esfahani, *Dar Khaane-ye Baradar: Panahandegan-e Afghanestani dar Iran.* Tehran: Research Institute for Culture, Are and Communications (RICAC), 2018.

11 https://www.aasoo.org/fa/articles/255.

12 https://twitter.com/fara_zamini/status/1582277977554923521?s=20.

13 https://www.afintl.com/202212207246.

14 Reported by *IranWire*, https://tinyurl.com/2uk4u5x8.

15 https://twitter.com/IranIntl/status/1637632549722759172?s=20.

16 Reported *by Shargh Daily*, https://tinyurl.com/52ys7ce2.

17 Reported by Fararu, https://tinyurl.com/3r63bk6x.

18 https://www.youtube.com/watch?v=_tthW9a0haQ.

8 I Give My Life for Iran: The Fight for Peace

1   https://www.radiozamaneh.com/754705/.

2   https://www.youtube.com/watch?v=2VfhFYU6G-k.

3   https://www.youtube.com/watch?v=LH6PH98NUuQ.

4   https://farsi.rouhollah.ir/library/sahifeh-imam-khomeini/vol/9/page/274.

5   https://web.archive.org/web/20090924040346/http://kayhannews.ir/880622/2.HTM#other200.

6   https://www.bbc.com/persian/iran/2009/09/090917_op_sepah_qods.

7 https://www.irna.ir/amp/7333064/.

8 https://www.youtube.com/watch?v=QqmkvTsH1FY.

9 http://www.rahman-hatefi.net/navidenou-557-89-390-891113.htm.

10 I've written a biography of Soleimani: Arash Azizi, *The Shadow Commander: Soleimani, the US, and Iran's Global Ambitions*. London: Oneworld Publications, 2020.

11 https://kayhan.london/1395/06/24/53072/.

12 https://www.zeitoons.com/104047.

13 https://www.aparat.com/v/BojDz.

14 https://thepeacefactory.org/israel-loves-iran/?doing_wp_cron=16921 89621.0364940166473388671875.

15 https://twitter.com/mostafatajzade/status/1211672239533383682.

16 https://twitter.com/arash_tehran/status/1619861426826547200?s=20.

17 Reported by Ensaf News, https://tinyurl.com/bdfn6y3k.

18 Reported by Ensaf News, https://tinyurl.com/3h8vt3y3.

19 https://www.bradford.ac.uk/alumni/notable-alumni/.

20 https://www.aparat.com/v/ohrdu.

21 Reported by Donya-e-Eqtesad, https://tinyurl.com/33ufvcwt.

22 https://www.magiran.com/article/2996587.

23 Reported by Afkar News, https://tinyurl.com/3fm5ntcb.

24 https://archive.org/details/20200707_20200707_1528.

25 https://www.youtube.com/watch?v=uNimrzpQleM.

26 Reported by *Etemad*, https://tinyurl.com/mtut4d75.

27 Published by the Embassy of Ukraine in the Islamic Republic of Iran, https://tinyurl.com/7akzruwj.

28 Reported by Iranian Students' News Agency, https://tinyurl.com/4p2vyjuw.

29 Reported by Fars News, https://tinyurl.com/4k7frket.

30 Reported by *Khabar* online, https://tinyurl.com/yetvz7rb.

31 Reported by *Bahar* News, https://tinyurl.com/5n7u6raa.

32 Reported by *Donya-e-Eqtesad*, https://tinyurl.com/mpn2k5ff.

33 https://ir.voanews.com/a/ukraine-russia-iran-war-protest-/6460722.html.

34 Reported by Didban Iran, https://tinyurl.com/yk3my7d7.

35 Reported by Iranian Diplomacy, https://tinyurl.com/2pjh9f47.

36 Reported by *Mardom Salari*, https://tinyurl.com/vbdww4zk.

9 Sarina's Revolution: The Fight for a Normal Life

1 https://www.radiozamaneh.com/734064/.

2 https://www.youtube.com/watch?v=Vzmc_O9w1Cc.

3 https://www.radiofarda.com/a/afsoon-najafi-hadis-iv-radio-farda/32054690.html.

4 https://www.youtube.com/@sarinacmz4015/about.

5 Reported by *Khabar* online, https://tinyurl.com/28y2wdyk.

6 https://www.youtube.com/watch?v=4f9G9n_9WkE.

7 https://twitter.com/Hozier/status/1578479749050925056?s=20.

8 https://tinyurl.com/m6nn7nkj.

9 https://www.youtube.com/watch?v=oaXA9c_DIrg.

10 https://www.youtube.com/watch?v=zy3fu20S26s.

11 https://www.youtube.com/watch?v=tmzGXOo4ZkY&t=1s.

12 https://www.youtube.com/watch?v=gpRnvFZ3vTU&t=1s.

13 https://t.me/sarinaez.

14 t.me/sarinaez2.

15 t.me/sarinaez3.

Index

Ramadan 9, 24, 176
Ramsar Sites 94
rape 135–6
Rashno, Sepideh 32–3
Rasoulof, Mohammad 117
Razavi, Davud 76
refugees 155–6, 159–64,
    169–71
  and protests 164–8
religion, *see* Bahá'ís; Christians;
    Islam; Jews; Zoroastrians
Reporters Without Borders 120
resistance 2, 28–33, 149; *see also*
    protests
retirees, *see* pensioners
Revolutionary Council 23–4
Revolutionary Guards Corps
    (IRGC) 27, 37, 57, 177
  and Bahá'ís 147–8
  and environmentalists 106, 108,
    109–10
  and Khamenei 212–13, 214
  and Syria 182, 183
revolutions 195–6, 206–8; *see also*
    1979 Revolution
Reza, Imam 10
Rezaee, Sahra 167
Riahi, Katayoun 113–16
Riazi, Maryam 16
Rida, Rashid 145
Roshangaran (magazine) 44
Rostaee, Sayeed 166
Rouhani, Hassan 83–4, 101, 211
  and the environment 102–4,
    105, 106
Rousseau, Jean-Jacques 195
Russia 182, 195, 211
  and Ukraine invasion 185,
    188–90
  see also Soviet Union

Saddam Hussein 26
Sadeghi, Arash 38
Sadr, Shadi 52
Saied, Kais 181
Salahsoor, Farajollah 114
Salarvand, Sepideh 167–8
Salavati, Abolqasem 108–9
Salesman, The (film) 117, 119
sanctions 68–9, 84, 211
Saqqez 5, 6–7
Sarvari, Mohammadreza 165
Saudi Arabia 8, 48, 109, 179
scarves, *see* hijab
Second Sex (journal) 46
Sediqqi, Kazem 30
segregation 51, 159–60
Seljuk dynasty 73
Semnani, Hossein 70–2
Sepehri, Mother 22
Seven Hills (Haft-Tappeh) 79–83
Seyed Emami, Kavous 107, 110
Seyf Khodro 66
Shah of Iran, *see* Mohammad Reza
    Pahlavi
Shahabi, Reza 76
Shahkarami, Nika 194
Shahrzad (TV series) 119
Shakoori, Bahman 135
Shamlu, Ahmad 27
Shargh (newspaper) 169–70
Sharia 15
Shariatmadari, Hossein 177
Shekari, Mohsen 117–18
Shia Muslims 134, 135, 142, 146,
    163–4, 179
Shirazi, Ayatollah Makarem 151
Shiri, Farahnaz 76
Shoemakers' Union 70–1
Shojaee, Mansoore 97, 99
Shojaee, Zahra 49

Also by Arash Azizi

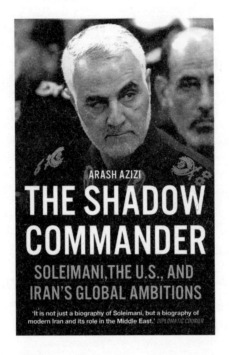

When the US assassinated Qassem Soleimani, he was one of the most powerful men in Iran. Known as 'the shadow commander', he enacted the wishes of the country's Supreme Leader across the Middle East, establishing the Islamic Republic as a major force in the region. But all this was a long way from where he began – on the margins of a nation whose ruler was seen as a friend of the West.

Through Soleimani, Arash Azizi examines how Iran came to be where it is today. Providing a rare insight into a country whose actions are often discussed but seldom understood, he reveals the global ambitions underlying Iran's proxy wars, geopolitics and nuclear programme.